Bringing up a Bilingual Child

Navigating the Seven Cs of Multilingual Parenting:
Communication, Confidence, Commitment, Consistency,
Creativity, Culture and Celebration

Rita Rosenback

Published by
Filament Publishing Ltd
16, Croydon Road, Waddon, Croydon,
Surrey, CR0 4PA, United Kingdom
Telephone +44 (0)20 8688 2598
Fax +44 (0)20 7183 7186
info@filamentpublishing.com
www.filamentpublishing.com

ISBN - 978-1-910125-24-3

Printed by CreateSpace

Illustrations by Tom Jones-Berney

I dedicate this book to the people in my life
without whom this book would not exist:

my late parents, Ritva and Egil,
who brought me up to become bilingual;

my dear daughters Minna and Daniela,
who are my inspiration, pride and joy;

and my loving husband Bob, who is my pillar of strength
and patient supporter in all that I do.

Testimonials

"Rita has become my go-to person in raising my children bilingually (French and English). Her straightforward advice, great ideas, and upbeat attitude, as well as her own success as a parent raising multilingual children, gives me the encouragement and motivation I need to keep on track with my own kids."

- Carol Callicotte-Belmon
Blogger at www.AFrenchAmericanLife.com

"You are holding a very special book in your hands: behind the clarity and depth of its content, this work is based upon years of experience and knowledge from the author. This turned out to be to priceless to me: this book, written by a mother of two children, will guide you through the entire path of multilingual parenting."

- Galina Nikita
Blogger at www.trilingualchildren.com

"Being bilingual is a major commitment that parents, teachers, caregivers and the social environment our children grow up in need to engage. Rita Rosenback gives a very detailed description of seven indispensable pillars for a successful bilingual upbringing of our children."

- Ute Limacher-Riebold
Blogger at www.expatsincebirth.com

"Rita is wise, mother-hen-gracious, kind and down-to-earth about dispensing advice on the joys and challenges of raising multilingual children. I would know – she's been a saving grace when I started doubting my own resolution of raising my son bilingual. She's not only a great resource, but like a welcoming friend ready to lend a helping hand."

- Rina Mae Acosta
Blogger at www.findingdutchland.com

Table of Contents

*"One language
sets you in a corridor for life.
Two languages
open every door along the way."*

- Frank Smith

1 Introduction

1.1 Who is this book for?

This book is aimed at (existing or soon-to-be) parents in families where more than one language is spoken. It is also written for anyone in the extended circle of family and friends of such multilingual families, as well as for anyone coming into contact with them. My wish is that my book will also be read by teachers, doctors, social workers, au pairs, nursery assistants, therapists and anyone with an interest in the topic.

This book is not written with monolingual parents raising a bilingual child in mind – that would be a different book. Although teaching a foreign language to a child in a family that only speaks one native language is in many ways similar to doing so with two or more languages, there are certain things that are distinctively different. Monolingual parents may still find this book helpful (and I am happy you are still reading), but please keep in mind that the target reader is someone in a multilingual environment. The decision to narrow down the target audience stems from my own experiences when I was looking for books on the topic. Quite often I would find myself frustrated to have to skip sections that were irrelevant to my situation or did not answer the questions that I had.

1.2 Presumptions I have made about you as a reader

In addition to the type of reader just mentioned, my main presumptions about you are:

- **You already think that it's beneficial to be able to speak more than one language**

    I will only briefly touch on the advantages of being a bilingual. There are, however, a few benefits that you may not have thought of, and those I will expand on in subsequent sections. In the *Confidence* section, I will also list the most common myths about bilingual speakers so you are aware of these. You will most likely encounter at least some of them, and it is good to have an answer ready when it happens. You can find a list of books and other sources of information on the advantages and myths about multilingualism in the *Resources* section.

- **You believe that parents can pass on their language(s) to their children**

  I will support you in your belief and boost your confidence in bringing up a bilingual child. I will share my family's story and provide you with advice, hints and tips that will help you create the right environment for your child to grow up acquiring more than one language. I will point you to further resources, of which there are plenty of.

- **You are not particularly interested in the underlying research behind multilingual families – you just want to give your child the best start in life as a bilingual**

  I will concentrate on the practicalities of multilingual parenting. This book is not a presentation of the research into multilingual families or the underlying strategies, nor does it contain detailed information on the linguistic development of children. Again, I will give you a list of books and other material on these topics for you to delve into, should you want to do so.

1.3 Aim of this book

The aim of this book is to help multilingual families to create a supportive environment for children in which they naturally grow up to speak more than one language.

The intention is to give you an easy-to-read-and-use guide to multilingual parenting. I want to strengthen your confidence in your own abilities by providing you with motivation, ideas, advice and answers to your questions.

Raising a bilingual child is not always plain sailing, but I am convinced that, with a little help, far more families would be capable of it than what is the case at the moment. I want this book to be your companion in bringing up a bilingual child. I hope it is going to inspire you when you feel less confident and give you further ideas while you are experiencing the joy of watching your child grow up learning to communicate. Perhaps it can also be the bridge to further books and other resources that you can find at the end of the book.

1.4 Who am I

I have waited to tell you about myself until now, as I believe it is more important for you to know what's in it for you. I was born into a bilingual family in the Swedish-speaking area on the west coast of Finland. My mother spoke Finnish with me and my father spoke the Finland-Swedish dialect of our small village, Dagsmark. I learnt my first "foreign" language at school, which is the so-called proper Finland-Swedish. When I was nine, I wanted to try the small Finnish village school, so I spent my third year at school with Finnish classmates. German, Finnish and Swedish were my main subjects at Åbo Akademi, the Swedish-speaking university in Turku in the south-west of Finland. I also spent one semester in Göttingen in Germany, studying mainly life, but also some German, Dutch and Spanish. After my studies, I first went on to work as a German teacher at my university, then as a translator, interpreter and editor for a travel guide. After moving to England in 1998, I have led multinational teams in IT and retail, and since 2012, I have concentrated on blogging at www.multilingualparenting. com and writing my book.

I am the mother to two adult bilingual daughters, Minna and Daniela, who were both born in Finland. Throughout the book, you will read about how they grew up become confident bilinguals. We still speak Swedish with each other whenever we are together, and with their father they continue speaking Punjabi.

1.5 Why I wrote this book

I believe that good communication makes life easier and better. The ability to communicate with people around you is a vital skill when you want to convey your needs, feelings and innermost thoughts, or even if you just want to ask for directions. The more and better people communicate, the less misunderstandings, regrets and disputes there are. If you can communicate in two or more languages, thereby crossing cultural and geographical borders and bridging generational gaps, you are positively contributing to increased understanding in the world.

Speaking more than one language is a way to enhance not only your own development and relationships but it also improves extended family bonds, intercultural understanding and acceptance. You learn new ways of thinking and become more open to new ideas and different cultures. I believe that if people all over the world communicated more and learnt more about each other, we would create a better place to live for ourselves and generations to come. However, let's start with changing our own surroundings before trying to solve the issue of peace on earth!

If you are a parent and have the opportunity to give your children the gift of communicating in more than one language, please don't miss this chance of a lifetime.

My two daughters, Minna and Daniela, have grown up to become bilinguals - Minna is fluent in four languages, Daniela in three. Our move to England added one more language to the mix, but already prior to that, having lived only in Finland, they fluently spoke three and two languages respectively (they were 6 and 13 years of age at the time of the move). Today, they are happy and confident to live or visit in England, Finland or India, feeling "at home" wherever they are. They have both also learned German at school and during their stays in Germany.

Since I moved to England, I have often come across families where more than one language is spoken, but the children grow up being comfortable speaking only the majority language. Several grown-up children from such families have told me that they are sad that their parents didn't insist on passing on their heritage language. They regret not having learnt the language at the time that it would have been so easy to do. On the other hand, I have never come across anyone regretting having learnt a language as a child.

With a linguistic and coaching background and having successfully raised two bilingual children, I want to share the knowledge I have gained and do so in a form that is accessible to anyone interested in the subject, not only to the ones who are used to reading books. From the outset, my goal has been to write a concise book for any family, and to do it in a simple, non-academic way.

1.6 How to use this book

How you should use this book depends on where you are on your multilingual parenting journey. If you are expecting your first child or your children are very small, I would recommend that you read through the whole book to prepare yourself for what the task of bringing up a bilingual child will mean for you and your family. As and when your children grow up, revisit the different sections to make sure you stay on track.

Of course, I invite every one of you to read all the sections, but I know how it is when you have children – when you have a question as a parent, you just want to have the answer straight away. If you are looking for something specific or just want to read about a particular topic, you can either check the **Table of Contents** for the subject or take a look at the list of questions towards the end of the book – there will be a reference to the relevant page where you can find advice relating to it. Because you can dip in and out of the book to find whichever topic you are interested in, what you will find if you read the book from start to finish is some repetition – I hope you will not find this too distracting.

You will notice throughout the book that I alternate between using the words 'daughter' and 'son'. This is purely to make the text flow better and to avoid having to use the pronoun 'it' (instead of 'she' or 'he') to refer to the neutral world 'child'. Also, I am using the word 'parent' for a person that is the main carer of a child – this could, of course, also be a grandparent, a foster parent or anyone else in charge of a child's upbringing.

Let's lift the anchor, hoist the sails and set off on our voyage across the seven Cs of Multilingual Parenting: *Communication, Confidence, Commitment, Consistency, Creativity, Culture and Celebration*.

2 Some basic stuff

2.1 Who is bilingual?

Depending on how strict in your definition of 'language' you want to be, the estimated amount of bilingual speakers in the world varies considerably. Most experts agree that the majority of the world's population speak more than one language. I subscribe to the revered linguist François Grosjean's definition of bilingualism:

Bilinguals are those who use two or more languages (or dialects) in their everyday lives.

I find this definition brilliant, as it

- mentions two or more languages, so everyone speaking more than one language is included and there is no need for distinguishing tri-, quadri- and-so-on-linguals or polyglots
- includes dialects and thereby avoids the question of defining the boundary between a dialect and a language
- emphasises the use of a language, not the fluency – being bilingual does not mean that you are fluent in the languages you speak

With the above definition in mind, the estimation is that more than 60% of the world's population is bilingual, i.e. bilingualism is the norm, not the exception.

I have chosen to use the term 'bilingual' for anyone speaking more than one language: 'my daughters are bilingual'. While I use 'bilingual' about individuals – independent of how many languages they speak – I will be using the term 'multilingual' to refer to ideas, concepts, practices and so on, e.g. 'multilingual parenting' and 'multilingual society'.

2.2 Advantages of being bilingual

As mentioned earlier, I will only briefly list the advantages of learning and speaking more than one language. Since you are reading this book, I presume I am preaching to the converted.

Wider communication
More languages equates to a larger number of people you can speak with in the family, community, at work and everywhere.

More conscious and sensitive communication
Not only can bilinguals speak with more people, but due to the awareness of differences between languages, they are more aware of what is being said and how to express themselves.

Increased cultural understanding
Knowing more than one language widens your understanding for other cultures.

Open mindedness
Generally, someone who has learnt more than one language and is also familiar with more than one culture is more open-minded towards new concepts, not only in a cultural sense, but in all aspects of life.

Enhanced thinking
Someone who speaks more than one language tends to think more in concepts than words. They know that one phenomenon can have more than one name. Different languages are also stored in different parts of the brain, thus developing those parts. Child bilinguals acquire the ability to understand how languages work at an early age, making it easier for them to speak about a language.

Improved selective attention
Children who learn more than one language early intuitively distinguish the relevant parts of spoken sound. They learn which

sounds are important for the meaning of what is said. This ability to block out unnecessary information and only pick up the relevant bits can also be used in other situations.

Improved memory
Research has shown that bilingual people have, on average, a better memory than monolinguals.

Increased creativity
Bilingual children have in tests been shown to be able to use creative thinking more extensively than monolinguals. This is thought to be a result of being used to seeing things from different perspectives.

Easier to learn another language
Once you know the structure of two or more languages, it is easier to generalise and learn an additional language or two.

Generally more successful in education
In tests, bilingual children have, on average, consistently scored better than their monolingual peers.

Better employment prospects
We have more international contacts than ever before in history. Having employees speaking the language of the country you are trading with is a distinct advantage.

Improved health
Recent studies have proven that bilinguals suffering from Alzheimer's disease can function better than monolinguals with the same degree of the illness, and that a bilingual person can stave of the illness by an average of four and a half years.

Increased self-esteem and identity
Presuming the parents have not only passed on their language, but also their culture, in a positive way, the self-esteem of the children will be improved and they will be more confident about their identity.

Knowing who you are and where you come from gives you a sense of security and increases your confidence.

Improved extended family unity in migrant families

When grandchildren can speak with their grandparents and other relatives "back home", this strengthens the family bonds and makes social interaction easier.

Parental authority (in a multilingual family)

If a parent does not know the majority language that the children use at school and with their friends, it is important that they can speak with the children in their own language and that the children can respond in the same language. Trying to get your message across in a language in which you are not confident rarely has the intended outcome. At certain stages in a child's development, it is important that you can be assertive and not leave yourself open to ridicule due to not having a common fluent language with your child.

Improved opportunities, more choices

Someone who can communicate in more than one language also has a broader range of choices: who to socialise with, where to live, what job to choose, where to travel, what literature to read, where to study, and so on.

2.3 Disadvantages of being bilingual

There are no known lasting disadvantages with being bilingual. In some cases, there might be a slight delay in a child's linguistic development, but the delay is temporary and the end result is well worth waiting for. Older studies which claimed to prove a delay in the language development of bilingual children have turned out to be based on inappropriate testing methods and assessment criteria. For example, a bilingual child who knew the word for two things in two different languages (= four words in total) was deemed to be lagging behind a child who knew the word for three things in one language (= three words in total). In any case, any disadvantage is by far outweighed by the benefits to you, your child, the family and the wider society.

Raising a bilingual child will present you with challenges that you will have to deal with as they arise. As a parent, you will have to put a bit more effort in and will need to stay alert and persistent during the phases when your child does not seem to want to know about your language. The more fluent you want your child to be, the more effort you have to be prepared to put in and the more attention you have to pay to your child's language development.

You may also encounter doubters, some of them professionals, who will try to discourage you from teaching your child more than one language. Being aware of these challenges ahead of time gives you a chance to mentally prepare and be ready for them. In the **Confidence** section, you will find advice on how to conquer your own and others' doubts.

*"If you talk to a man
in a language he understands,
that goes to his head.
If you talk to him in his language,
that goes to his heart."*

- Nelson Mandela

3 Communication

Why start with communication? Isn't that what should be the end result, your child being able to communicate in more than one language? Yes, but to reach this admirable goal, a child's parents have to communicate with each other to clarify their goals. If you are a single parent, go through the same thought process. It is important that those closest to the child know what they want the outcome to be. If you don't know where you are going, it is difficult to find the way.

You have to keep in mind that although your daughter grows up in a multilingual family, it does not mean that she will automatically pick up all the languages and actively use them. She may end up understanding but not wanting to speak a particular language. There is no point in trying to force her to speak a language, it will not work in the long run. Instead, make a conscious decision to raise her to naturally become bilingual.

Once you have agreed your goal for passing on your language to your daughter, communicate your decision to the grandparents, extended family, friends, nannies, day care professionals and teachers, as well as anyone else she comes in to frequent contact with. You may want to involve some of these people, especially her grandparents, at an earlier stage, while you are still establishing your goals, as you might need their support along the way.

Be aware that your decision to raise your little girl to be bilingual may be questioned by some people around you. They will have different reasons for doing so and, as a result, you may feel that your decision might not have been a wise one after all. Therefore it is important to prepare yourself with answers to all the reservations you might encounter.

The most difficult doubts are those coming from people you would normally fully trust and whose advice you would readily take in any other situation. These reservations might come from your parents or parents-in-law, who may have misguided conceptions about how a child learns languages and what effect it will have on the overall development of their granddaughter. Your daughter's teacher might discourage you from teaching her any other language than the majority language. The family GP may indicate that she could be negatively affected by the use of several languages and that you are doing her a disfavour. Or in the worst case scenario, your daughter's speech therapist may tell you that your family's use of many languages is the reason for the delay in her ability to speak clearly/her dyslexia/ stutter or any other speech related impediment.

This is what happened to my family. Our younger daughter Daniela was a late speaker; she didn't string an intelligible sentence together until she was about three and a half years old. This didn't worry me too much, as I knew that children develop at a different pace. We were, however, referred to a speech therapist by the efficient Finnish child health screening process and also had to take an EEG which required my three-year-old to sit still for 30 minutes without falling asleep or paying attention to anything specific (I should have had a medal!). The tests came out absolutely fine but the speech therapist was adamant that it was the use of multiple languages in the family that had confused Daniela and that she might be permanently disadvantaged if we didn't stick to one common language.

Since we were already using three languages in the family, I knew only using one would never work, but the therapist's advice did stop me from teaching Daniela Finnish. Thus she learnt to speak only two languages while we lived in Finland, when her elder sister picked up three. Thankfully, the desire to learn Finnish stayed with Daniela, and she has attended Finnish classes at university. She has noticed that she does still have a good passive knowledge of the language and that her pronunciation and accent are significantly better than those of her fellow students.

You will be pleased to know that these reservations, no matter how well-meant, are based on myths and incorrect information. In the **Confidence** section, you will find the reasons why they are wrong and why you are right to stick with your decision.

If you find yourself wanting further back-up for your decision, I recommend that you speak to other parents that have successfully brought up their children to speak both (or all) of their family's languages. Also visit my website at www.multilingualparenting.com to connect with other like-minded families.

To have the confidence to meet others' reservations about your decision and to be able to explain it to others, discuss and prepare the answers to the following questions – each of which will be the topic of a section to follow:

1. Why do you want your child to learn your language?
2. What level of fluency do you want your child to have?
3. What strategy will you be using to raise your child to be bilingual?
4. When will you start teaching your child the language?

Once you have answered these questions, you are ready to start creating your own unique *Family Language Plan*, which will be the topic of the last part of this section.

3.1 Why raise your child to be bilingual?

Since you have picked up this book and are still reading it, I presume that you have already made up your mind to pass on your family's languages to your son. You are already convinced that knowing more than one language will be a great advantage to him and also to you, the family and the society as a whole. You may even have thought of benefits other than the ones mentioned in the **Introduction**.

There are, however, some things that you may not have thought about, and those are more to do with yourself and your feelings. Ask yourself the following questions and write down your answers. Putting the answers in writing is important, because it will force you to complete your thoughts and form coherent sentences. I assure you, seeing your thoughts and feelings written down on a sheet of paper has a surprisingly strong impact.

At first glance, the questions will seem very similar, but read them carefully, preferably aloud, and answer each question exactly as it is phrased. You will be amazed at how much this process of questioning yourself clarifies your thoughts (by the way, these four question types can be used when making any decision):

1. What happens if I bring up our child to speak my language?
2. What happens if I **do not** bring up our child to speak my language?
3. What **does not** happen if I bring up our child to speak my language?
4. What **does not** happen if I **do not** bring up our child to speak my language?

As long as you are honest in your answers, there are no right or wrong ones. Do give as many answers as come into your mind for every question. Make sure to list both the pros and the cons. The answers you give will vary depending on your own and your family's situation, but they are the right ones for you. Please do the above exercise now, before continuing to read, as I am about to give some example answers, which I don't want to influence your own thoughts.

Possible answers to the four relevant questions:

Question 1: *What happens if I bring up our son to speak my language?*

- He will be able to speak with his grandparents and other relatives in their language
- We can speak my language together
- He will be able to easily get along in more than one culture later in life

- Knowing another language will be an advantage to my son in his career
- He will gain all the benefits of being bilingual
- I can tell him the stories I know from my childhood in my own language

Question 2: *What happens if I **do not** bring up our daughter to speak my language?*

- My parents will have difficulty in understanding what their granddaughter says
- She will need someone to translate for her when meeting relatives
- I might regret my decision later in life, and then it will be more difficult to pass on my language
- It will be clear who speaks what language to who in the family
- My daughter might resent me for not teaching her my language
- It will be harder for her to learn the language later on

Question 3: *What **does not** happen if I bring up our son to speak my language?*

- There won't be any communication problems when we visit my home country
- My son will not have to learn the language later in life when it is much more difficult and time-consuming
- I don't have to worry so much about the family unity breaking down, even after I am no longer around
- He does not have to feel ashamed about not knowing his family's language
- I don't have to explain to my son why I didn't speak my language to him
- He won't feel left out in conversations with my relatives

Question 4: *What **does not** happen if I **do not** bring up our daughter to speak my language?*

- She will not fully appreciate the richness of my culture and its traditions
- The bond between my daughter and her grandparents may not be as strong
- She will never thank me for giving her the gift of another language
- I will not be able tell the stories from my childhood as vividly in a different language
- My daughter will not be mixing her languages
- I will not be offering my daughter all the advantages an additional language can give

I truly hope you answered the questions for yourself before reading the above examples. If you did, you would have come up with some additional answers that are unique to you and your family. You may also have come up with some reasons that you weren't aware of previously.

Keep the paper where you wrote down your answers, as you will need it when you complete your *Family Language Plan* later in this section.

3.2 Level of fluency

Part of your decision making and goal setting process is to determine what level of fluency you want your daughter to have in the languages that you are passing on. Keep in mind that the higher the level of fluency you want for her, the more effort you as a parent have to put in to reach the desired level.

The majority of the world's population is bilingual, but it is rare to be fully fluent in both or all of your languages (see the list of myths about bilinguals in the **Confidence** section). It is actually an exception for bilinguals to achieve a native level of fluency in all their languages.

When deciding how well you want your daughter to be able to speak your language, you must be realistic. Think of what you want to achieve, and again, discuss this with the other parent, as you should agree on what you are aiming for to avoid disappointment in the future. There are no guarantees you will achieve the level of fluency for your daughter that you would like, but you can certainly make sure you create the best possible language environment for her. On the other hand, you may be surprised how well it all turns out if you are prepared to put effort into supporting her learning.

Not only should you think about how well you want your daughter to be able to communicate in the language, also think of whether you want her to be able to read and write it. I would strongly recommend that you include at least reading into your goals, as this will open up a whole new world of experiences in the language and will also help her to enhance her language skills. When it comes to reading and writing it makes a difference whether both languages use the same script. If the alphabet is different, learning to master the minority language reading and writing skill will require additional support. Unless you are confident that you will have the ability, time and persistence to teach her yourself, it might be worth looking at, for example, weekend schools or other activities, if available in your language, courses or even investing in some private tuition.

On the following page is an example list of communicational fluency levels to help you decide at which level you would like to aim for your child. Note that someone who knows a language and its grammar perfectly but hesitates to speak it would belong in either the 'adequate' or 'limited' level, so this list is not about an academic proficiency level. The crucial factor is how well someone is able to communicate and how willing they are to do it. The list also gives you an indication about what kind of support you would need to be able to achieve the different levels:

Speaking and understanding

1. *Native or bilingual fluency*
    A native or near native (fully fluent bilingual) speaker means that
    you have full command of the language and speak it with no or
    only a slight accent, noticeable only to other natives. Experts say
    that to achieve this, you would need to start learning the language
    before the age of six and have plenty of exposure to it. If you start
    to learn the language at a later age, you would need to make a
    conscious effort to learn to speak accent-free. You are generally
    also able to read and write the language.

2. *Confident communicational fluency*
    You know the language and feel confident to speak it with a
    native speaker. You have an accent, but it is not so strong that

it would make what you are saying difficult to understand. You would achieve this growing up in a multilingual family where the minority language is consistently used and you also have other opportunities to communicate using the language. You feel motivated to speak the language and have a positive attitude to it. You know how to read and write, or would at least be learning to do so.

3. *Adequate communicational fluency*
    You are able to speak the language, but prefer to use the majority language. You can get along in daily life using the language, but you don't feel fully confident in doing so. Compared to native speakers, you feel more like a foreigner learning the language, but your attitude towards it is positive. You can understand some of what you read.

    In particular, teenagers from multilingual families, who were confident communicators in the language at an earlier age, fall into this category when their lives revolve more around school, hobbies and friends than the family. Without support and motivation, their use of the language may become limited.

4. *Limited communicational fluency*
    You can understand most of what is said, but can only answer in simple sentences. You switch to the majority language as soon as the opportunity presents itself. If it was your choice, you would avoid speaking the language. Due to lack of practise or motivation, you don't feel confident to speak the language.

5. *Passive understanding (also called 'receptive knowledge')*
    You can mostly understand what is said, but don't feel able to answer in the same language. You don't attempt to take part in conversations in the language, unless there is an urgent need to or you get a strong motivation to do so.

Reading (and writing)

You can read text written in the language and possibly also write yourself. As with the speaking ability, there are, of course, different levels of reading and writing ability, but I will not go into more detail about these as there are too many variations depending on the family language combinations. The amount of time needed to learn to read (and write) also varies dependent of whether there is a whole new alphabet to be learnt or not.

Based on the above, think about what level you want your daughter to be at when growing up. Note this down in preparation for your *Family Language Plan* document.

You now know why you want your daughter to grow up learning the family's language(s), and you have decided which level of fluency you would like for her. Next, you need to decide which communication strategy you should choose for your family.

3.3 Choose your communication strategy as a family

By now, I hope you are convinced that bilingual (or even multilingual) communication is a good choice for your family, and you want your son to grow up speaking more than one language. You know why you are doing this and now you need to know how to go about it all – what approach should you use?

There is no one-fits-all solution, and you may be disappointed to hear that there is no foolproof way of guaranteeing that your son will learn all the family languages. However, there are strategies that will give him the best possible environment in which to naturally grow up to become bilingual.

Be aware that although consistency is one of the cornerstones of successfully raising a bilingual child, family circumstances may change

– and they often do. A second child, the move to another country, the loss of a major source of language support, your son starting school, a divorce or change in preferences due to some other factor, may require you to review your choice of strategy. If this happens, be open-minded and remember to keep your son's best interest in mind and not persist in a decision you made in the past.

The main approaches multilingual families use are:

1. One parent, one language – OPOL
2. Minority language at home – mL@H
3. Time and place
4. Mixed use of language

The list is not exclusive, and there are families who have come up with their own unique strategies. Many families use a mixture of these during different phases in the family life. The main thing to know is that it is always the outcome that matters, *how* you got there is, in the end, not important. The strategy itself has no value unless you achieve the goal you set for yourself and your son.

To allow you to make an informed choice about what fits your family best, I will next briefly explain the different strategies.

3.3.1 One parent, one language – OPOL

This is probably the most widely used approach for multilingual families. In the past, it has also been claimed to be the only right way. *One parent, one language* is a great strategy but not the only way to achieve the goal of bilingual children. The abbreviation OPOL is widely used for this strategy.

As the name indicates, *One parent, one language* means that each parent speaks a different language with the child. The language may or may not be the parent's native language, though preferably it would be. When addressing their child, the parents are consistent in their use of language. They might even go so far as to switch language mid-sentence, if that part of what is said is aimed only at the child.

The first question that arises about *One parent, one language* is which language to use when both parents are present – which language should be chosen as the common one when all the family is together. To make this easier to explain, I need to bring in the terms of majority language and minority language. The majority language is the main language of the society the family lives in. It is normally also the language of the education system – the nurseries, schools, universities and so on. A minority language is any other language only a smaller part of the population uses, or even only one family. It might, however, be the main language of one or both sides of the extended family. Note that the description of the languages will change if the family moves to a region with a different language setting.

The answer to the question of which language should be the common one for the family depends on the following:

1. Which language each parent can speak
2. Which language is less spoken in the child's environment

If the parents have only one language in common, this will normally naturally become the main language of the family, be it the majority or minority language. It can, however, also be a third language, which the parents have chosen to speak to each other, maybe before they had children. In this case, the child will learn one language from each parent and gain at least a passive understanding of the parents' common language. The child's fourth language will be the one spoken in the community.

Where there is more than one language in common, the recommendation is to choose the one that the child will get least exposure to as the language the family speaks when together.

In families where one of the parents does not speak the minority language and the family speaks the majority language when together, it is vital that the minority language parent takes every opportunity to speak his or her language with the child. The minority language parent should preferably use his or her language in *all* direct communication with the child. This, of course, requires an agreement between the parents. The majority language parent has to accept that sometimes the minority language will be spoken even when he or she is present.

A majority language parent with a positive attitude towards the other language is vital in supporting the child learning the minority language. Such a parent will normally also pick up words and phrases along with the child and will at least gain a certain level of passive knowledge of the language. The added bonus is that the majority language parent will also be able to understand more of the discussions in the extended family and feel less left out during family visits when the main spoken language is the minority language.

Without realising and certainly without any conscious effort on my side, I picked up some Punjabi – a language I knew nothing about prior to meeting the father of my daughters. This happened just by me hearing the conversations between my ex-husband and our girls. I had a grasp of the common phrases used with regards to meals, shopping, playing and so on. However, I had more knowledge than I realised, which came to light when I stayed for a long holiday with my eldest daughter Minna at her grandparents' home in India. Almost everyone in the family spoke English, so I could get on well. My mother-in-law and my daughter's 114-year-old great grandfather, however, didn't, and I very much wanted to have one-to-one conversations with them. There was nothing else to do than to try to speak, so I did. More to my amazement than theirs, they seemed to understand what I was trying to say and I was able to speak with them directly without anyone translating. What a wonderful feeling it was! My Punjabi must have been absolutely awful, but the connection with them was so much more intimate and rewarding.

Don't be afraid to use the minority language even if you might feel that you don't know it perfectly and you might be missing some vocabulary. Presuming your little girl will hear the minority language from other speakers as well, she will not adopt the mistakes you make, or if she does so initially, she will correct herself when hearing others use the right word or grammatical form. What will happen is that your own command of the language will improve as your daughter learns it.

How well you can communicate with your daughter is extremely important for how well you connect with her. Don't use the minority language if it makes you feel uncomfortable, but find another way of passing it on. Language is important, but not at the cost of your relationship with your daughter. However, do give it a try for at least a couple of weeks before you give up on the idea of passing on the language yourself. If you have access to grandparents or other relatives or friends, they will most likely be more than willing to be of assistance. Remember to give them the advice found in this book, though.

As mentioned, if you choose a language that the other parent does not understand, I can't emphasise enough how important it is to discuss and agree about this in advance. You don't want to find yourself arguing about the family's language – there are enough things to worry about in a young family as it is. The other parent will have to accept that his or her daughter might initially use words he or she may not understand. Without such an agreement, the situation may turn into a power struggle between the parents, which is not what you want in a family.

If the exposure to the minority language is relatively low, it is strongly recommended to choose it as the common language for the family. This may feel strange to start with if the parents have so far been speaking the majority language together, but stay with it, the reward of doing so is that your daughter learns the language far quicker and she will also continue using it with you while being exposed to the majority language at the nursery or school. Don't worry too much about the majority language – she will definitely become fluent in it later.

Experts generally agree that a child needs to be exposed to a language for more than 20%, ideally 30%, of their waking time to pick it up. However, our family's experience shows that it can be done with less. It may just need a little bit more consistency on the minority language parent's part and support from the other parent in finding ways for the child to spend time in surroundings where the minority language is spoken.

I would recommend that you do the maths: who is your daughter going to spend time with during the first six or so years of her life? If the *One parent, one language* method does not provide enough exposure, and you can't find the necessary support elsewhere, you might want to consider the *Minority language at home* approach instead, if it is viable.

When choosing which language to speak with your daughter, ideally choose the language you feel most comfortable with. Think of which language you would rather express yourself in if you wanted to describe something exciting or interesting. However, go for the language you feel most passionate about – you can pass on a language even if you are not fully fluent in it.

3.3.2 Minority language at home – mL@H

The *Minority language at home* approach does what it says on the tin: both parents speak the minority language at home. The child will learn the main language of the society from others: relatives, family friends, nannies, playmates – if not before, then by the latest in nursery or at school. Don't be concerned if your son does not know the majority language by the time he goes to school – he will learn it soon enough. The abbreviation mL@H is often used for this strategy.

The *Minority language at home* set-up is more straightforward than *One parent, one language* and has a lot going for it in that there are no choices that have to be made with regards to who speaks what language to whom in the family. Both parents speak the minority language and the child will learn the majority language from other sources.

The big concern parents have with regards to the *Minority language at home* approach is that their child might be disadvantaged when going to school not knowing the majority language. There has been much research into this and always with the same result: though children who don't know the majority language will initially not be able to follow the teaching, they quickly learn enough to understand what the teacher says. They reach the same level as their peers in a short amount of time and when measured at key stages of their education, they on average perform better overall than their monolingual classmates.

My own experience, as well as those from other families that have used the *Minority language at home* method, consistently confirm that the child learns the majority language from other children or at the nursery, or at the very latest at school.

When we moved to England, our younger daughter Daniela was six years old. She was a late speaker, so had only spoken something we could understand for less than three years. Daniela did not know any English when we arrived, and as you start school two years earlier in the UK than in Finland, she was due to go straight into year two.

The school agreed to let her start in year one, and for about three weeks she didn't understand much of what was going on, but she was highly motivated and had great support from the teachers and other pupils. Within about a month, she could tell us what had been happening at school during the day, and after three months she started to speak English. She was *moved to her age-appropriate class and we put some extra effort in to help her with her writing. Her late start with English has in no way been detrimental to her development at school: in year five she got the "Best Speller" award. Daniela achieved an A* in her GCSE English and has gone on to study medicine.*

Children brought up with the *Minority language at home* strategy tend to get a solid foundation in the minority language and are less likely to switch to the majority language when speaking to their parents. Using the home language will become second nature to everyone in the family, and even though siblings among themselves at some point might switch to using the majority language between them, they will still use the "right" language when speaking to their parents.

The *Minority language at home* approach is to be recommended especially in cases where there would otherwise be little or no exposure to the minority language for the child. A typical situation would be that a family moves to another country with a different language: everything is new and the family might not have any relatives close by. They are yet to make many friends with others speaking their native language and don't visit their home country that often. Both parents do speak the new country's majority language, but neither of them fluently. The absolute best option for the family in this case is the *Minority language at home* method. The family will keep a strong bond by using their native language. A move to another country causes a lot of stress for a family and it is important that the family unity stays strong. The children will get a solid foundation in their language and will soon learn the language spoken in the "outside world". Small children don't care if another child can speak their language or not – if they want someone to play with, they will find a way of communicating. It is fascinating to see how quickly they can interact and come up with games and even rules for their play without a common language.

For my elder daughter Minna's wedding, we were fortunate to have relatives arrive from all over the world, among them the five- and seven-year-old daughters to my niece from Finland who speak only Swedish; and the four-year-old daughter of relatives in England, who speaks English and Punjabi. They didn't know how to speak with each other, but it only took a smile and a reached out hand from one of them before they were all off together onto the dance floor. They had great fun together all evening and played a running-around game which seemed to follow some rules. Had they had a chance to stay a bit longer together, I am sure they would have started to teach each other words of their respective languages. Where there is a will, there is a way.

I know it can be a bit of a leap of faith to be confident that your son will learn the language of the community well enough to successfully participate in school life and learn alongside other children, but multiple examples speak for this strategy, especially with children under seven years of age.

If your son is a bit older, maybe a teenager, you can take a slightly different approach as his native language is already well established. If both parents know the majority language and he is willing to participate, you could use the *Time and place* (see next section) method to practise the language in the family instead of *Minority language at home*. If only one parent is confident in speaking the majority language, you could consider *One parent, one language*.

Whichever method you use, remember that the minority language is the one that will need most support to remain an active language for your son. Once at school, the majority language will be the prevailing one for him and he might want to switch to use this language at home as well. The more consistent the use of the minority language has been up to then, the easier it is to maintain it as an active language between you.

3.3.3 Time and place

Families that find that neither *One parent, one language* nor *Minority language at home* is suitable for their specific circumstances, but who still want to have a structure for how they communicate within the family so that the family's languages can be passed on to the children, may want to go for the 'time and place' approach.

As the name indicates, the parents choose a time and/or a place when/where they speak a specific language. This approach works best with slightly older children that are able to e.g. associate a room in the house with a language or to know that on weekends the family only speaks a certain language.

The plus point of this strategy is that it allows the parent to more easily control the amount of exposure to each language, depending on which language is in need of more stimulation and increase the exposure time if necessary.

Whilst proven to be successful when applied consistently, this strategy requires more concentrated effort and commitment from both parents than *One parent, one language* or *Minority language at home*. The parents have to vary how they speak with their children depending on the time of the day, the day of the week or where they are. I have heard about a family that taught their children two additional languages by dedicating different rooms in their home to different languages. This is certainly admirable, but you need a lot of focus if you want to pass on your languages this way.

Besides being more difficult to implement, this way of learning the language may make your daughter reluctant to use the language at a different time or in a different place. As the aim is to bring up children that can naturally communicate in more than one language, this approach is not the first one I would recommend. The artificial nature of the rules in this strategy also make them more likely to be broken.

Another drawback is that while this strategy may be successful within the family, once your daughter gets more influenced by the majority language at nursery or school, she is likely to prefer it as a means of communication. It may well happen that she one day wants to use only the majority language, having spoken different languages according to the family rules up to then. Children that are used to their parents switching between languages when talking directly to them are more likely to give up use of the minority language than those who have always only used one language with their parent.

3.3.4 Mixed use of language

When applying the 'Mixed use' method, bilingual parents use both (or even all) of their languages when they communicate with their child. The parents use whichever language feels right at any time. The choice of language can be dependent on the topic, who else is present, how they are feeling or where they are. This method is easy to put in place, and you don't have to plan or think which language to use. The mixed use approach requires less effort, but the outcome is also less certain.

Your son will most likely pick up both languages as long as he also hears the languages separately from other people speaking only that particular language. It is important that he learns to distinguish the languages from each other.

The strategy may work well, especially if both (or all) of the spoken languages get the necessary confirmation and boost from other exposure. However, research has shown that the more a parent mixes the languages used with the child, the greater the chance that the child will drop the minority language when starting school and peers become more important. Due to the lack of rules, and as soon as the child feels that it is acceptable to use only the majority language, the likelihood is that this is exactly what will happen and it becomes more difficult to keep up the minority language use at home. Children in families where parents are consistent in their language use are more likely to become bilingual as adults.

There are several success stories among *Mixed Use* families, so it is certainly doable. However, since the research shows that the success rate is lower, my recommendation would be to choose either *One parent, one language, Minority language at home* or *Time and place* as you are more likely to succeed in achieving your goal with these strategies.

3.3.5 Mixture of strategies

One parent, one language, Minority language at home and *Time and place* are the main strategies that families use to bring up bilingual children. However, what you will find is that in most cases families end up using one main approach interspersed with some of the others.

> *This was the case with our family, We started as a* One parent, one language *family with me speaking Swedish and the girls' father talking his native language, Punjabi, in a mainly Swedish-speaking community in Finland. When we moved to England, we maintained the same language pattern, but became a* Two minority languages at home *family.*

The important thing is to be aware of what is working and, if necessary, adjust the *Family Language Plan* to suit the circumstances. Always keep in mind that the goal of bilingual children is the important bit, not how you got there.

3.3.6 Single parent family

Single parents *can* bring up bilingual children. I know some experts discourage single parents from attempting to raise bilingual children, as it is not an easy task. Things to take into consideration are: Will you be the person passing on the minority language? If yes, how much time will you be able to spend with your son? Will sticking to the chosen language cause extra pressure for you? I am stating the obvious here, but being a single parent is not easy at the best of times, so you need to be realistic about what you can take on. There are a lot of benefits in becoming bilingual for your boy, but a highly stressed-out parent due to additional pressure from the chosen common language is a very high price to pay. However, if you feel passionate about it and, after taking the above into account, feel it is doable, I also believe that you can do it and commend you for it. It will take a fair amount of determined commitment, a lot of your time, some help from others and maybe a bit of money, depending on the circumstances.

As with two-parent families there are also different language set-ups for single-parent families. Each scenario will need its unique approach.

Bilingual, single parent

If you speak two languages (one of which is the majority language of where you live) and want to pass both of them on to your son, the best (and arguably easiest) option is to speak the minority language with him, as per the *Minority Language at Home* approach. Although you know both languages, it is better to only speak the minority one with him, as this is the one he will be less exposed to. Your boy will learn the language of the community in nursery or school, by the latest. He won't use the language with you, so don't be fooled if he doesn't display his language skills at home. Keep in close contact with the school so you know how he is progressing.

If you speak two minority languages and want to pass them both on, then it is recommended to set some structure to how you speak the languages with your child using the *Time and place* strategy. You can alternate languages based on time (e.g. every other day, week or fortnight) or place (e.g. at home and outside the home or different rooms of the home). A word of caution though; this is a tough regime to follow, and you need to be really committed and determined to go through with it.

Monolingual, minority language single parent

If you move to a different language environment with your child, you might find that you are the only person that regularly speaks your language with your little boy. You will most likely be working, so the time you spend with him is restricted to evenings and days off. Should you give up on your language and support your son in learning the local language? The recommendation is not to give up your language. A solid foundation in the home language is the best support for learning an additional one, so the advice is to keep speaking your familiar language with your son. So you would effectively be using the *Minority Language at Home* strategy. A move is a big change for both adults and children, and changing the language you have communicated in until would only add to the pressure. Should you switch to the majority language, it is highly likely that your son would gain at most a passive understanding of your language.

Depending on how old your son is, there are different ways you can support him. A child under the age about seven will pick up the local language fairly quickly once immersed in it in nursery or school and grow up to speak the language accent-free. You can prepare your little one by watching children's programmes and cartoons in the language together before the move. If he is a bit older, look for online tuition, some of which you can find for free on educational and governmental websites. The more costly option is to enrol him in a language course or to arrange private tuition.

Monolingual, majority language single parent

What to do if your son has had a bilingual start in life and you become his sole carer and don't know the minority language he is still learning? In this scenario, you will need some help from others to keep the minority language active in your son's life. Try finding a way to create a similar scenario to the *One parent, one language* system. If you still have a good relationship with the other parent's family, ask them to support you by spending time with your boy and helping you with materials such as books, magazines and DVDs. If this is not a viable option, look for a childminder who can speak the language, possibly an au pair. Try to arrange play dates with other children speaking the language. If your boy is a bit older, also look for weekend or evening classes in the language. If you are lucky, there might even be immersion classes available at your local school. What you could also consider, is to learn the language alongside your son – I know, not an easy task to take on, but something you might want to think about if you are truly passionate about retaining the language.

Finally, even if all doesn't quite go as planned, don't be hard on yourself. Remember that some additional language skill is still a lot better than none – a receptive knowledge (passive understanding) of a language is a lot easier to turn into an actively used one than learning a language from scratch.

3.4 When to start?

By now you have decided and discussed your decision to raise your daughter to speak your family's language(s) and you have also chosen the approach you are going to take. You have also decided on the desired level of fluency. So when should you start your "project"? The answer is simple: Now.

It does not matter at what stage of parenthood you are, whether you are expecting your firstborn or have become the proud parent of the world's most wonderful baby – start now! Perhaps your daughter has said her first word or she is attending a playgroup, enjoying the time with other children. Maybe you are looking forward to your second child and want to bring in another language to the family. Your girl may already be at school or even in her teens. Whatever the situation is, the answer to the question of when you should start speaking your language to her is: Now.

It is never too late to start, but the earlier you begin, the easier you will find it. Also keep in mind that bonding with your baby is probably more enjoyable if you can do it in your native language. You are also more likely to know children's rhymes, songs and stories in your own language – the ones that you were told when you were small. For example, you will instinctively know how to make animal noises in your own language.

In addition, the longer you wait before you start talking to your daughter in your native language, the more difficult the switch from one language to another will be, not only for yourself, but certainly for her. The language you speak is closely related to your identity. To experience such a drastic change in a parent will cause resistance if a child is already used to speaking a different language.

Our eldest daughter Minna learnt Finnish from me and Punjabi from her father. When she was about five, I decided that now was the time for me to start teaching her Swedish as I wanted her to attend a Swedish-speaking school. Minna was generally a calm and sweet girl, but oh, the tantrum when I tried to switch from speaking Finnish to using Swedish with her. She was not having it and got extremely angry with me every time I tried. What a conundrum and disappointment for me – I had not thought it would be an easy change, but never had I imagined that her reaction would be so strong. I was, however, determined that she would learn Swedish, I just had to get over the threshold of introducing the language to our relationship.

The solution presented itself in form of a kitten, something Minna had wanted for a long time. So we found a kitten, but not any kitten, it was a Swedish-speaking kitten! With all the honesty of a parent telling the children about Santa Claus, I explained that it would be cruel of us not to speak Swedish to the kitten, now called 'Pricken' (Swedish for 'spot', which it had on its nose). We had taken Pricken away from his mother, which must have been traumatic for him, so we shouldn't make it more difficult for him by speaking a language he didn't understand. Minna fully agreed and asked me to speak Swedish to Pricken as she wasn't able to. So I found myself translating between Minna and her kitten – never has a little cat been spoken to as frequently as Pricken! Unfortunately, Pricken disappeared after about six months (maybe he wanted some peace and quiet), but Swedish stayed as an accepted language and when Minna was seven (the age at which children start school in Finland), she went to the Swedish-speaking school.

Contrary to what you may have heard or read, there is no hard and fast age before which a child has to start learning a language to be able to speak it well. Children of any age can learn to master a language. Research has shown that the only major difference is that children that have learnt a language before the age of six usually end up speaking the language accent-free. You can still learn to speak without an accent if you acquired it later in age; it just requires more of a conscious effort.

To support your daughter's learning process, communicate with her as much as possible. Speak a lot, about anything. To get used to this, it is best if you can start when you are expecting – each partner speaking the language you have chosen. When your baby is small and not yet able to speak, tell her what you are doing, describe the things around you. Sing, read stories, rhymes and poems - the more she hears you speak, the easier it is for her to learn the language. This way, your language also becomes an integrated part of your relationship with her. When your daughter starts to speak, engage her in a conversation whenever the opportunity arises – it doesn't matter what age she is or even if you don't understand what she is saying. Answer all those 'Why?' questions. Pay attention to the tone of your voice – she should feel that you are genuinely interested and want to communicate with her.

3.5 Creating the Family Language Plan

It is important that you create your own unique *Family Language Plan* so that it is clear in your own mind and for everybody involved what you are aiming at, why you are raising your son to be bilingual and how you will get there. Having a clear goal will ensure that you stay on track and know if any part of your plan is not going as expected. The plan will also help you in times of change when you need to adjust your chosen approach.

At the end of this book, you can find a template for a *Family Language Plan,* which you can copy. You can download a bigger template from www.multilingualparenting.com/FamilyLanguagePlan. Complete the form with the information specific to your family and situation. If you are bringing up more than one child to become bilingual, make a separate *Family Language Plan* for each child.

Part One: Reasons why

In this section, write the main reasons why you want your son to become bilingual. If you answered the four questions in chapter 3.1, then you already have a list. If you didn't answer those questions, I would recommend that you go back and reread that section and do the exercise. The answers will be your main reasons. Once you have your list, read through it and think whether you have any other motives that drive you to want your son to speak the chosen languages.

Part Two: Level of fluency

In Table A, write the level of fluency you would want for your son. You can reread chapter 3.2 to remind you of the different levels. Define the levels for each one of the languages separately. Keep in mind that the higher the level of fluency, the more effort you need to be prepared to put it and the more attention you need to pay to arranging enough exposure for him. For each language, also note down whether you want your boy to learn to read and write in the languages he is learning to speak. If your plan has more than three languages (including the majority language), remember that the general rule of thumb is that for a child to acquire a language while growing up and become an active speaker of it, the recommended exposure time is 30% of the child's waking time. This is, however, only a guideline and fluency can be achieved with less exposure.

Part Three: Strategy and Exposure

Step One: Choose a strategy

Based on the descriptions of the main different strategies in chapter 3.3, note down which one you have chosen for your family's circumstances. There will be times when you may be using a mixture of the strategies, but to achieve as much consistency as possible, I recommend that you select one of them to be your main approach.

Step Two: Exposure

Independent of which strategy, or mixture of strategies, you have chosen, fill in Tables B, one for each language. Write the language in the top left corner of each table. In the left hand column, write the names of the people or places or the time providing the language exposure. Then fill in the hours per day for the whole week, add the hours up and enter the number in the last column on the row. To see how much exposure your son gets per day per language, you can also do the sums on the bottom row of each Table B.

Transfer the totals from the right hand column of each Table B to column (A) in Table C. In column (B), write the amount of time your son is awake per week, on average. This means, for example, that if he sleeps nine hours a day, you are left with 15 hours of waking time each day. Times this by seven and you have the total amount of waking hours for the week, which would be 105 hours for the example used. Enter this number in column (B) for each language. If you haven't used a calculator until now, you might want to do so in the next step, as you should divide the sum in column (A) with the sum in column (B) and enter the result in column (C). To get the amount of exposure as a percentage, times the number in column (C) by 100. If you like formulas, it's (A)/(B) x 100 = %.

Although I have created these tables to enable you to have a realistic view of how much exposure your son gets for each of his languages, remember that this is not a definitive guide for whether your son can acquire a language or not. If you notice that the exposure level for a language which is not the majority language of the community is getting low, let's say well under 30%, and you are unable to increase the exposure time, there are other things you can do. Make every minute count when he is getting the exposure. You can replace watching cartoons with reading a book and discussing what happens in the story. Make any interaction in the language engaging. Have fun and create memorable moments in the language. Also note that once your son has become confident in speaking a language, the need for daily exposure is decreased. However, to keep the language alive, keep talking!

Part Four: Support

Once you have filled in the first three parts and tallied up the amount of exposure you estimate your son will get for each language, you might find there is a shortfall for a language, or that you are struggling to reach the desired time each week. If this is the case, then take a look at the support network around you – family, friends and other multilingual families. Can they help you in achieving your goal? Even if you find that the amount of exposure is spot on, it is always good to have thought about additional people that could come to your aid should you need it. If you need to find more ways to get language exposure for your son, write this down as a task.

Part Five: Materials

Do you have books, magazines, films and other materials that will be of help for your son when he is learning your language? If not, think about where you could find them. Of course, you can always make up your own fairy tales, but in the long run it is definitely easier to have some books to read at bedtime. If you need to stock up on language materials, write this down as a task.

Date

At the end of the form, enter the date when you completed the form. When the time comes to update your *Family Language Plan*, you can download a new one from www.multilingualparenting.com/ FamilyLanguagePlan.

What to do next?

By now I hope you have definitely made up your mind to bring up your daughter to speak your family's languages. The advantages this will bring to you, your daughter and the whole family are clear to you. You have discussed your goals within the family and let relevant other people know. The decision about which approach you are going to take has been made so you know who will speak what language with whom, where and when in the family. You have an idea on how fluent you want your daughter to become. You have also made up your mind about when to start – which I hope is: Now. With all these decisions made, you have the components of your unique *Family Language Plan*, which you can collate into one document with the help of the template, which you can find at the end of the book.

This means that you have now embarked on the great voyage of bringing up your daughter to speak your language. You have already successfully navigated the first C, the one where you start and which will also be your ultimate goal: **Communication**. Maybe you have felt that it has been plain sailing in familiar waters to you and you really didn't need to look at the chart. Now we need to prepare you for the rest of the journey, equip you with all the tricks and tools you need to avoid the shallow grounds, tackle stormy waters and make it through any lulls on the journey. The next C on your chart is: **Confidence**.

*"Confidence is contagious.
So is lack of confidence."*

- Vince Lombardi

4 Confidence

I am absolutely 100% confident in your ability to raise your child to speak your language.

Read that sentence again.

How can I, someone who doesn't even know you, be fully confident about something that you may doubt yourself. Well, I do, because if you follow the advice of this book and stay confident in your own abilities, you will succeed, no matter what you or anyone else may think right now.

You need to have confidence in:

- your ability to pass on your language
- your child's ability to learn the language
- the advantages to you, your child and all the family

The first thing you should realise is that you already have all the resources you need to succeed in bringing up a bilingual child. Nothing can stop you, except yourself by not believing that it can be done. You can do it, and you have made the right decision. Even if you feel that you don't speak the language "well enough" to teach it to your child, you can still do it. There are plenty of other people who will be happy to help and resources that will strengthen your daughter's language.

Secondly, you need to know that your little girl has the capacity to simultaneously learn to speak more than one language. This has been proven both through research and in the millions of families that have already done it. A child who can learn to speak one language, can learn to speak two, three or even more. If you suspect that your daughter might have a language disability of any sort, then pick this up with a specialist. However, choose someone who is familiar with multilingual families, so you get the right advice.

Just to boost your confidence a bit, read through the advantages of bilingualism in section 2. With all these benefits to be had for your daughter: social, emotional, educational, professional and even physical – what better gift could you give her?

Rest assured that in a few years' time, you will have forgotten any extra effort you had to put in. The overall feeling will be pride – in what your daughter, yourself and your family have achieved. The extended family will be delighted and she will be thankful for your efforts – if not now, then certainly later in life. It will all be more than worth it in the end.

In the next chapter, you will find out about the importance of your language for your confidence as a parent. Taking into account that more than half of the world's population speaks more than one language, it is amazing how many myths there are about bilingualism. You will learn the truth about these myths, so that you can confidently counter them. You will also read about circumstances where your confidence might be put to the test and how to deal with these situations.

4.1 Using your most confident language with your child

To be a parent is a demanding task, and choosing to do it using more than one language does make it a bit more challenging. As a parent, you need to have endless love, caring and patience; you have to be a good role model and sometimes you need to be the authority setting the all-important boundaries for your son. When he is at risk of doing something that might be dangerous or hurtful to him or others, you take it on yourself as a parent to use your authority to stop this from happening.

Speaking your own language makes you more confident when expressing your innermost feelings. The right words for telling your son that you love him; phrases with which you console your daughter; expressions of joy and encouragement – these all come a lot easier to you in your native language.

Imagine yourself in some of the following situations:

- Your 8-year-old, football-mad boy is not selected for the school football team and comes home broken-hearted – what words do you use to comfort him?
- Your girl's friend has all of a sudden decided she doesn't want to play with your daughter anymore – how do you console her?
- For your birthday, your little boy has written a poem about how important you are to him – how do you express your love to him?
- Your little daughter is learning to swim and is afraid to go in the water – what words of encouragement do you say to her?
- You have found out that your son has skipped some lessons at school to go out on the town with his friends – how do you tell him to attend school regularly?

Let's pick up on the authority side of parenting. As soon as your son understands spoken commands, you show your authority through your speech. If the words you are saying don't come easy to you since you are not speaking in your native language, your authority may suffer. Surely it is more about what you say and not how you say it, you may think, but when you have a confrontation with your teenage son, you don't want to give him a chance to comment on *how* you say something. Teenage years bring out new sides in your son, sides you never thought existed. Thankfully this is a phase that passes, I should hasten to add. When it is time to show your authority, your confidence is more important than ever. Make sure you can use your most confident language in these situations.

There are parents who only revert to speaking their native language when they need to assert their authority, providing their child understands their language, of course. This is understandable, since it is difficult to express your strongest emotions in a language you don't fully master. It is, however, also sad if the only situation where you use the language closest to your heart with your son is when you are upset or angry. What kind of feelings about the language would that teach him?

Being confident about your language identity comes with a positive attitude towards the language. Once you have a positive attitude, you automatically convey this to your son. He will pick up on it from your behaviour and language use, and it will rub off on him. He will grow up cherishing the language, just like you, and he will feel confident to use it.

Being used to speaking your most confident language with your son will also make it easier to stick to it when he, influenced by his school and peers, wants to switch to speaking the majority language with you. All this said, if based on what type of strategy you have chosen for your family, one of you does end up speaking a less confident language, merely being aware of the above will make the task easier to tackle.

4.2 Myths to be aware of

One of the definitions for the word 'confidence' is: *The state of feeling certain about the truth of something*. What an excellent definition, knowing the facts about something gives you confidence. Being aware about the myths makes you prepared to stay confident in what you are doing.

Along your multilingual parenting journey, you will come across many experts, real or self-proclaimed, who want to give you advice about what you should and shouldn't do, and what may or may not happen. Taking into account how many people in the world are bilingual, it is astonishing how many myths there still are about learning more than one language or about bilingual individuals in general. There are myths by the dozen, and in this section I will briefly describe 36 of them. You need to be aware of these common misconceptions, so you know how to identify and confidently respond when they are presented to you disguised as facts:

- 9 myths about language
- 9 myths about bilingualism
- 9 myths about bilingual parents and multilingual families
- 9 myths about bilingual children

When someone talks to you about these myths, I suggest one of two approaches: If the person is willing to listen (and hopefully learn something), then gently but confidently inform them of the actual facts. On the other hand, if the person is someone who won't change their mind, or you don't have the desire to explain the same thing for the umpteenth time, then simply politely say, "Thank you. I will think about that". Then forget about it and resolutely change the topic of the discussion. Bringing up your child to be bilingual is your decision and it is your right to ignore anyone trying to convince you differently.

4.2.1 Nine myths about language

There are many myths about languages in general and these nine are just a start:

1. **Myth:** *Some languages are better than others*

   In some families, there seems to be a perception that their family's language is not as "good" as, for example, English. For this reason, they may decide not to pass the language on. They might also think that a language will be of no use to the child in their career later on in life. There are no "good" or "bad" languages; every single language has its own unique properties and will most certainly be useful.

2. **Myth:** *Some languages are more difficult than others for children to learn*

   A normal child will always learn the family's language, independent of how "difficult" other adults perceive the language to be. Children *acquire* their first language(s). They don't learn them in the same way as adults. For a child, no language is more difficult than any another to learn.

3. **Myth:** *Foreign influence on a language should be resisted to keep a language "clean"*

   Throughout time, languages have always been influenced by each other. What people today may think to be a "pure" language is actually something that has evolved over a long time, and continues to do so. We may think that the language we spoke as children was the "correct" language and that it is all going downhill. A language will always change and no two generations will speak exactly the same.

4. **Myth:** *Today's language is sloppy*

   This is related to the previous myth. Just because the language is changing, it does not mean that it is any worse than what was spoken 50 years or so ago. It is simply different – funnily enough, every generation has complained that young people can't speak and write properly anymore.

5. **Myth:** *Everybody speaks English*
    Whilst English is an important language in today's world; and English is spoken more or less everywhere where English-speaking people live or travel, it doesn't mean that you will be able to get along only speaking English. Even if you do, all you do is "get along". You can't connect with the people and the culture in the same as if you spoke their language. This applies both in your personal as in your professional life. Selling something to a customer is a lot easier if you can do it in their language.

6. **Myth:** *Adults can't learn a new language well*
    Untrue. We don't lose the ability to learn a language. In the right circumstances, anyone can learn a language and even become fluent. There is no age limit to language learning. Adults normally do just not have enough time (and motivation) to be successful at learning a new language.

7. **Myth:** *You have to learn the grammar first*
    To uphold the motivation to keep studying a language, the opposite is true. When you notice that you can express yourself in a language, you want to know more about how to construct your sentences. Also, once you get better at a language, the grammar makes much more sense and does not feel like a chore any more. You notice that it strengthens your language and gives you more confidence in using it.

8. **Myth:** *A country needs to have a single language not to fall apart*
    I wonder what the Swiss, Canadians, Indians and Finns would say about this? There are several countries in the world that have successfully integrated more than one language into their country's identity. This myth is often used by politicians with underlying reasons for stating their concern about their country's "proper" language.

Confidence

9. **Myth:** *Immigrants don't want to learn the language*
    There are very few immigrants who don't want to learn their new host country's language. It seems that these individuals exist first and foremost in people's minds rather than in real life. There may be those who don't learn the language well due to not having the opportunity to study it or having insufficient exposure to it, but it doesn't mean they don't *want* to learn.

4.2.2 Nine myths about bilingualism

These nine myths are among the most common ones mentioned about bilingual individuals in general:

1. **Myth:** *Bilingualism will delay the learning of a language*
    Research has shown that there is no difference between the speed at which monolingual and bilingual children learn to speak. There are differences in which order bilingual children learn aspects of the language and therefore may be diagnosed as developing late when tested using criteria designed with monolingual children in mind. There are early and late speakers in both groups. If a child has a specific language related difficulty, the child would have it independent of whether the child learns one or two (or more) languages.

    My family is a good example of early and late talkers. There was more than two years' difference between the age when Minna started to use longer phrases and the age when Daniela put together her first sentence.

2. **Myth:** *Real bilinguals have acquired their languages early in life*
    In the right circumstances, anyone can come a bilingual at any point in their life. The fact that you might not have started to speak your language to your children from when they were born does not mean that they can't pick it up later.

3. **Myth:** *Bilingualism means being fully fluent in both (or all) of your languages*
    It is highly unusual that someone is fully fluent in all languages they know – one will almost always be stronger than the other. The fluency can also vary during different times of one's life depending on how much exposure there is to the language. This may change due to a move to another country, a new partner, a new job or hobby or some other alteration in circumstances.

4. **Myth:** *Real bilinguals have no accent*
    Having an accent in the language you speak does not mean that you are not bilingual. Experts reckon that if you have learnt a language after the age of six or seven, you will most likely have an accent in your speech, the degree of which will vary depending on many factors. But anyway, most people, bilingual or not, have some kind of an accent when they talk. Not to have an accent is unusual.

5. **Myth:** *Mixing languages is a lazy way to talk*
    When bilinguals talk with each other, they often mix their languages. For someone listening to such a discussion, this may sound odd, shabby or plain wrong, or at least as a very lazy way of talking. Not so; a lot of research has lately gone into how bilinguals mix their languages and the phenomenon has its own name: *code switching*. Experts have found that mixing languages is a highly developed skill, with strict rules on what can be mixed when and how. Bilinguals switch from one code (i.e. language) to another for certain reasons and only with people that will understand what they say.

6. **Myth:** *Bilinguals have split personalities*
    Speaking more than one language does not mean that you are somehow "split". You do have more than one language to communicate in, but this does not divide your personality. This myth is normally presented by monolinguals who closely link their own language with their personality and then think anyone

who speaks another language, or even several, must have a split identity. Yes, language is linked to your personality, but speaking more than one does not split it – the two (or more) languages become an essential part of your identity as a whole.

7. **Myth:** *All bilinguals are also bicultural*
Being bilingual does not automatically mean that you are bicultural. You can speak a language fluently but still not feel that you belong to two different cultures. Language is very important for a cultural identity, but on its own it is not enough.

8. **Myth:** *Bilinguals can easily translate between their languages*
Being able to translate from one language to another is a specific skill that takes time to master. Knowing two languages does not mean that you can easily translate between them. Never take for granted that a bilingual can quickly (and without being paid) translate a text for you!

9. **Myth:** *It is unusual to be bilingual*
Well over half of the world's population uses more than one language in their everyday life and is, by definition, bilingual.

4.2.3 Nine myths about bilingual parents and multilingual families

The misconceptions about bilingual parents and multilingual families are also rife:

1. **Myth:** *A parent must know his/her language excellently to pass it on to a child*
Anyone who can speak a language can pass the language on to their child. You don't need to be an eloquent speaker that never makes any mistakes. Neither do you have to be an academic or someone with a high IQ. Have confidence in your own abilities, spend time with your children, speak, read, sing with them and watch them grow up to become bilinguals.

2. **Myth:** *Parents will pass on mistakes they make in their language to their child*

    Experts have found that any language mistakes that children pick up from their parents, they will quickly correct when they come in touch with other speakers of the language who don't make the same mistake. What seems to happen is also that children start pointing out these mistakes to their parents, thus improving their language as well.

3. **Myth:** *A child will naturally become bilingual as long as they regularly hear both languages*

    Only hearing both languages does not make a child bilingual. Learning a language requires interaction with others, speaking as well as listening. Children who hear two languages but are spoken to in only one would normally end up fluent in one language and have a passive understanding of the other, i.e. they would be able to understand but not speak it. Children are not like sponges and don't automatically learn any language they hear around them.

4. **Myth:** *Speaking a different language at home will have a negative impact on children when they go to school*

    Naturally, children that don't know the language spoken at school will initially need more time to get to grips with everything. However, research has shown that these children quickly catch up, learn the language and go on to achieve better grades than their monolingual peers. If parents don't know the language of the school, they may want to arrange for someone else to help the children with their homework when it is needed. This is more of an issue for the parents than the children, though.

5. **Myth:** *'One parent, one language' is the only right strategy to bring up a bilingual child*

    While *One parent, one language* has its advantages, it is not the be all and end all of approaches. It might be the only sensible option in certain families, e.g. where neither parent speaks the other parent's native language. Also, if there is enough exposure to both languages within the extended family, among friends and in the society, it is a good option. However, if the parents speak a minority language which the child will have limited exposure to, the *Minority language at home* strategy is to be recommended.

6. *Myth: Once you have chosen one strategy, you must stick to it, no matter what*
    While consistency is important when bringing up a bilingual child (more about this in a later section), circumstances change and you may have to re-evaluate the choice of strategy. Moving abroad, another child, a divorce – there are several reasons why you might have to review your decision. Do what is best for your child's development. Don't be rigid in your ways. Changing a strategy does not mean you have failed in what you tried to do; you are simply looking for the best possible option.

7. *Myth: You should **always** correct a bilingual child's mistakes*
    Be wary of correcting a child's language, especially if the language is not yet fully evolved. Negative feedback is not what you want your child to associate with talking your language. In the **Consistency** section, you will find ways of dealing with such situations.

8. *Myth: You should **never** correct a bilingual child's mistakes*
    Once a child is more confident about the language, you can advise on the correct pronounciation/word/grammatical form and so on, as long as you don't make a big deal out of it. If you notice that it discourages your child from talking the language, wait until he or she is more confident.

9. *Myth: All children in a multilingual family will automatically grow up with equal language skills*
    Children are different and have varying experiences both in the family, at school and with friends. It is not the same to be the middle child compared to being the firstborn, for example. Children are interested in diverse things and learn differently. A child who is keen on reading will most certainly have a larger vocabulary

than someone who likes painting more. All this inevitably leads to their language skills also being different. If you want all of your children to become fluent in your language, keep a close eye on each of them. One sibling may need more support than others at certain stages in their lives. Note that this applies equally well to monolingual children and their language development.

4.2.4 Nine myths about bilingual children

Bilingual children also get their fair share of incorrect assumptions:

1. *Myth: Only linguistically gifted or clever children become bilingual*
   This is probably the myth that annoys me the most, and I know it has stopped parents from even trying to pass on their language to their children. Everyone learns to speak, with the exception of a few individuals with specific disabilities. Acquiring a second (or third) language as a child is no different from picking up the first one. The point is that in the right environment, children *acquire* their languages, they don't learn them. There might be those that pick up a language more easily than others, but the same goes for any skill – some children may not be as good at maths or sports, but it doesn't stop them from doing well at school or enjoying a game of football. Your child doesn't have to be extraordinary in any way to learn your language ... yes, I know, we all have extraordinary children, but you know what I mean.

2. *Myth: A child should know one language properly before learning another*
   The earlier children start to learn another language, the better. Research has shown that there is no difference in the age at which bilingual and monolingual children start to speak, so there is no need to wait for one language to develop before introducing the second one. As a matter of fact, the earlier a child learns to speak a language, the greater the chance of an accent-free pronunciation (as long as the language is regularly used). Experts agree that if

you learn a language (from native speakers) before the age of seven, you will usually not have an accent in that language.

3. **Myth:** *Speaking more than one language in the family will confuse a child*
    Small children quickly pick up what belongs to which language. They don't learn a jumble of sounds and words. They soon instinctively know how to distinguish and reproduce language specific sounds – a skill that we seem to lose as we get older. If parents speak different languages (*One parent, one language* approach), children identify one language with their mother and the other with their father. Staying consistent in the language use will confirm the child's knowledge of the two languages. However, even when parents mix languages themselves, children will eventually learn to speak a "clean" language, as soon as they get exposure to it from other speakers.

4. **Myth:** *Bilingualism has a negative effect on a child's overall development*
    Some people think that learning two languages as a child "takes away" brain power and the child's overall development slows down. This is wrong on so many levels. A human brain has an enormous amount of processing power and it is like a muscle: the more you use it, the more powerful it gets. Research has shown that different languages develop in separate parts of the brain to some extent. These parts are also used for other purposes such as, for example, the ability to pick out relevant sounds and shut out unnecessary information. The ability to switch from one language to another enhances a part of the brain which is called the executive control. This area of your brain is among others also responsible for the ability to stay focused on a task.

5. **Myth:** *A child has to learn a language before the age of seven to become fluent*
    You can become fluent in a language at any age; the difference is how much effort you have to put in. With the right amount of

exposure and support, anyone can become fluent. Adults rarely have the chance to immerse themselves in a new language environment in the way that a child experiences it when growing up in a multilingual family. Also, the later you start speaking a language, the stronger your accent will be. So if you have the chance to give your child the gift of an additional language, there is no time like early childhood.

6.   **Myth:** *Bilingual children will always mix their languages*
     When learning a language, bilingual children sometimes mix in words from their other language. This phase will soon pass, and they learn to distinguish their languages. They will learn to only use words from the other language when speaking with people who know both languages. Bilinguals talking with each other almost always mix their languages (*code switching*), but they are also very apt at changing their behaviour to suit monolinguals when necessary.

7.   **Myth:** *Learning more than one language at the same time can make a child "semilingual"*
     This myth, which indicates that a child will not learn any language properly, is closely related to the previous one about mixing. This is not true; a normal child growing up in a multilingual family and spending time with other speakers of the language will learn a language appropriately.

8.   **Myth:** *Watching quality TV programmes is a good way for a child to learn a language*
     While a helpful support for the language development, children's TV programmes and digital media can never surpass the effectiveness of human interaction. For a child to learn effectively, the language exposure needs to be two-way and practical. Your child will learn the names of different clothing much more effectively if you repeat the words while emptying the washing machine, than by watching the best-made animation about the different pieces of clothing.

9. **Myth:** *Children learn some languages more easily than others*
    Children will learn whichever language they are spoken to by the
    people they grow up with. Just because an adult may perceive
    one language to be more difficult to learn than another doesn't
    mean that it would make it any more complicated for a child. A
    child picks up a language differently to how an adult does – it is
    more a process of acquiring the language of your environment
    than to consciously learn it.

4.3 When your confidence is put to the test

Your confidence may be put to the test in many different ways. You
may question yourself and your ability to go through with the task
of bringing up your daughter to become bilingual. Others may make
you doubt whether you made the right decision. What about school?
What will happen then, and how will other pupils and teachers react
to it all?

Then there is the biggie. You've made your decision and you've
spoken your language to your daughter; everything seems to be going
fine, no problems at school, but all of a sudden you notice that she
responds to you in the "wrong" language. What happened there?

In this section, I will delve into how to tackle such situations and I
will start with the one where your little girl may answer you in the
"wrong" language, as this is something that several parents have said
is the toughest hurdle of them all.

4.3.1 Your child responds in the wrong language

Getting a response in the "wrong" language from your child is one of
the more difficult situations facing a parent in a multilingual family
and also one of the most common reasons for giving up on raising a
bilingual child. After all, it is so easy to give in, especially when you

are also battling with all the other pressures of parenthood – why add another stress factor to the mix?

So why does this happen and how should you react? There are several reasons which depend on the child's age and environment. The start is easy, a baby will accept whatever language you speak. This is also the time when you should get used to speaking your language with your son – it is harder to switch a language at the point when you hear his first precious words. Parents speaking two different languages should become the norm well before the child starts speaking. This way you have language patterns in place when the communication becomes more interactive.

The patterns may get shaken up when your son goes to a play group, nursery or school. He notices that other children and adults speak only one language – he sees a different norm than the one used at home. The second critical phase is when he becomes a teenager and – in true style for many children of this age – knows best and doesn't have time to listen to you.

Small children

So you have followed all the recommendations, made sure that you have spoken your language for enough time to your daughter and everything has been maybe not always easy, but at least successful in the sense that the language of communication between the two of you has been the one you chose. Then she starts nursery and all of a sudden, there is a big change. She starts speaking the "wrong" language to you.

The first time this happens, you are probably taken aback, disappointed, not knowing what to do. You may even doubt your ability to go through with bringing her up to be bilingual. You question yourself about where it all went wrong. At this point, take a deep breath and relax. This happens in most multilingual families and it can feel disappointing and exhausting. All kind of emotions are welling up inside of you, but in no way is it the end of the road.

Children are generally very pragmatic in their behaviour and the same goes for their language use – whatever feels easiest. What you have to do is to steer your daughter back to using your language. This does not mean that you are being a horrible strict parent (no matter what others say). If your daughter wants to eat sweets all day, you stop that as well, because you know what is best for her.

When your little girl speaks the "wrong" language to you, it is important to not change your own language use. At the same time, it is also vital to stay calm and not make a big deal of the situation. Use gentle coercion, repeat what she said, but in your language. Lead her towards the "right" language by asking questions "Did you mean…?", "Oh, I see, you saw …", "What happened when …?" Listen carefully and show your joy when you get the response in the "right" language. Some parents use the method of pretending not to understand, though I would be careful with that approach, as you may be accused of not telling the truth when she hears you speaking the language to someone on the phone.

Consistency and persistence in language use are crucial, but they may not always be enough. You need motivation both for yourself and your girl. For her, use bribery, tricks, whatever works to get over this phase. Buy an action figure or hand puppet that only speaks your language, sing songs, read stories, make up games in your language. Make speaking your language fun.

Another important factor is to always be proud of your own language and show it. Your attitude towards your language and culture will rub off on her. For yourself, keep in mind all the advantages the additional language will bring with it – and by all means, reward yourself with something nice each time you manage to stick with it. But don't come blaming me for any extra weight you put on because of all the chocolate biscuits…

Teenagers

By the time your son has grown up to become a teenager, you have long lost the right to choose his clothes, hobbies, friends, what food he eats and which TV programmes he watches. Language is no different, I am afraid. If he sets his mind on speaking the majority language, you need to tread carefully to get him back on track speaking your language. Unless you want to have a major rebellion on your hands, using pressure or commands is not the way to go. Depending on your son's personality, he may speak the language because you tell him to, but if there is no real reasoning or motivation behind that, you may be doing more harm than good to his future as a bilingual.

What you need to do is to try to figure out what makes your teenage hero rebel against speaking the language that you have so successfully communicated in up to now. You also need to be realistic about it – it is another phase you need to have the confidence to get through. Teenagers can reject anything that they have fully embraced before, including a language.

Take every opportunity to explain why you find it important that you continue speaking your language. Your son may accuse you of being far too strict, old-fashioned, embarrassing, misguided – you name it, he'll throw it at you. There are also other reasons than teenage rebellion that cause your son to change his language with you. As with any other teenager, he may feel a strong peer pressure to conform. He wants to be like everyone else and not stick out of the crowd by speaking a different language. This may lead to him asking you not to speak your language when his friends can hear. If this happens, don't insist on speaking your language in public, but continue to do so within the family.

Minority languages are sometimes perceived to have a lower status than the majority language, due to the speakers of it being less affluent members of society. This may become a reason for your boy to think that it is not worth keeping up the language he learnt as a child. Make sure you clearly show pride for your language and heritage. Explain to him what it means to you and the rest of the family. If possible, arrange an extended visit to monolingual relatives to allow him to appreciate what he would lose if he would not be able to communicate with them. Make sure these visits are fun and don't add to the reluctance to speak the language.

Teenagers can also be very sensitive about not wanting to exclude anyone from a conversation. Your son may feel that it is rude to speak a language that not everyone understands – so he responds to you in the majority language. Again, go with the flow and don't cause a scene – never demand that he speaks your language in front of his peers. For teenagers, parents can be embarrassing enough by just being present.

Gentle persuasion, explanation – several times over and most of all, providing motivation on your teenage son's own terms are the ways to get him to keep your common language alive. Be the patient parent with the long-term vision. Experience has shown that once this phase is over, the young man your tantrum teenager has turned into will be ever so grateful for your persistence.

4.3.2 Have confidence in your own abilities

No one can undermine your confidence as quickly as you can do yourself. To avoid this, you need to arm yourself with all the facts about the advantages of bringing up your daughter to become bilingual. In addition, not only do you need to know the myths and how to dispel them, you also need to prepare yourself in case you start to question your own abilities when you are faced with some of the rough seas along your journey.

A good way to boost your confidence is to think back and see how far you have already come – in a later section, you will find ideas on how to keep a *Language Success Diary* of your daughter's progress. Read it to remind yourself of your successes. Another way is to think forward: find a quiet place, close your eyes and imagine yourself and your daughter in ten years' time, fluently speaking your language with a close relative or friend. Immerse yourself in that thought, describe to your inner self how it feels, what it sounds like, what you and your girl are saying, what others are commenting about you as a multilingual family, how proud you are. Stay in that moment for a while and memorise the feeling. Do this exercise before continuing to read.

A wonderful emotion, isn't it? Now think about the years leading up to that moment; what did you do to get there? What steps did you take? Which choices and decisions did you make? How did you react? Think all the way back to this moment and whatever makes you feel less confident right now. Ask yourself what you need to do *now* so that you can later, in real life, experience the emotions you felt looking into the future. You will know what to do to regain your confidence.

In the next chapters, I will go more closely into some of the more common situations which might cause you to waver in your decision. You might be worried that you will not have the time and energy to pull through and that you would rather not even try than to experience a failure. Perhaps you think that you don't know your language well enough. Maybe the status of your language in society is not that high and you think it might be more of a hindrance than a help to your daughter. Maybe you are a single parent and don't know where to turn for help. Read on.

What if I will find it too hard?

Being a parent to small children is stressful as it is. Having more than one language in the family can surely only serve to increase the stress levels. Well, it does and it doesn't. Of course, there are times when you would like to use the same language as others to make life easier.

You are explaining something to your inquisitive four-your-old which your partner already did but in the other language, while your six-year-old is telling you in the "wrong" language that he doesn't want to go to school – well, it could drive even the calmest parent close to the brink. Then again, reading the same stories to your daughter as your mother read to you, hearing your son chat away to his grandparents and sing a song you knew as a child – these occasions will absolutely make your day.

Don't be too hard on yourself if you occasionally slip into the wrong language – but don't allow it to become the norm. If it does happen, afterwards take a bit of time and think about why it did. Why was it easier for you to use the "wrong" language? What could you do to prevent it happening again?

If you frequently find yourself thinking that it is all too hard, discuss the situation with someone other than the people you have around you every day. Get in contact with a parent who has been successful at raising bilingual children. You could, for example, put up a post in the forum on www.multilingualparenting.com to find support and advice from other parents and experts.

If you feel that you don't have the energy to put in all the effort that is needed to give your son enough exposure to the language, ask for help. Speak with relatives and friends to arrange some quality time for your son with them. Maybe you can offer to have a monolingual family's toddler for the afternoon and later on get an afternoon off in return. The main thing is, don't be too hard on yourself and don't think you have to do it all on your own.

What if I don't know my language well enough?

If you are a parent and a second or later generation immigrant to a country or a speaker of a lesser used indigenous language, you may have concerns about your own knowledge of the language you want to pass on to your children. Maybe the language use in your family

Confidence

while growing up wasn't that consistent. After starting school, you may have used it less and less. Now, as an adult, you may have the feeling that you don't know the language well enough and perhaps you are not too sure what to do.

Don't worry, you can still do it. You don't need to have perfect command of the language you want to teach your daughter. Initially she may pick up some of your mistakes, but as long as you see to that she also spends time with other fluent speakers of the language, the mistakes will disappear. Soon enough, you will find yourself corrected by your daughter, who will get immense satisfaction from doing so. As her language evolves, yours will improve as well.

Even though your language use may not be perfect, the exposure to it is crucial for your girl's learning. There is a general consensus among experts that for children to naturally become bilingual while they are growing up, they should ideally be exposed to the language for 30% of their waking time. This time does include being in a group where the language is spoken, watching TV programmes or DVDs, listening to stories or music and so on – it does not mean they have to be interactively using the language for *all* that time, but human interaction should make up the majority of the exposure. Watching children's programmes in the language will on its own not be enough. However, a child can learn a language with less than 30% exposure – this has certainly been the case in my family.

To increase the amount of exposure to a language, don't be afraid to encourage other adults to use it with your daughter (even if the others are also bilingual). Explain why you want them to speak your language and you will find that most people (especially grandparents) are more than willing to help. Be warned though; it will most likely take a few reminders from you, if they have already started speaking a different language with your child. Switching the language you speak with someone – child or adult – is never easy.

Reading is an excellent way of supporting both your own and your daughter's language. When she is a small baby, it does not matter what you read: a magazine, cookbook, your favourite novel or an article on renewable energy – you name it. Anything to get you into the habit of reading to her is good. Later on, you will notice that stories and fairy tales do keep her attention better, but choose ones you enjoy yourself as well. As every parent knows, you will be reading them over and over... and over again!

My language has such a low status in the community, why bother?

Even though your language may not be as highly appreciated by the community as the majority language, it does not make it any less important for your family. There are no "good" or "bad" languages; every language is valuable and has the ability to enrich a person's life and their view of the world. If you think that your language is not important, find out more about it. You will discover an abundance of wonderful literature and stories, which would be so much harder to fully comprehend in any other language.

Also think of the reasons why some people might claim that your language is not as important as the majority language. Is it actually the language these people think of, or do they have some other motive? Speaking one language doesn't take away from learning another, on the contrary. Knowing your family's language and heritage also makes you feel more confident about your identity. Being aware of who you are makes you stronger and more able to deal with other people's prejudices.

I am a single parent – will I be able to do it?

I take my hat off for you for wanting to raise a bilingual child, even if you will have to carry most of the responsibility for it on your own. Please read chapter *3.3.6 Single parent family* for advice and ideas on how to go about it.

My daughter has been diagnosed with ASD. Should we stick to the majority language only?

Researchers have not found any evidence that children with Autistic Spectrum Disorder in families with more than one language would benefit from one of the family languages being dropped. In fact, the likelihood is that the opposite is true as dropping a language would mean a big change in the day-to-day life of the child and in a *One parent, one language* family it might negatively affect the relationship with the parent whose language would no longer be spoken. In a *Minority language at home* family, everyone would have to change their language use, which would be an even greater upheaval. For any child, a strong foundation in the home language is also vital for learning the majority language.

4.3.3 Others putting doubts in your mind

What to do when you feel that you know what you are doing, know how to go about it, but then others makes you question whether you have made the right decision? A particularly difficult situation is when parents are not agreed on what language(s) their child should speak. Grandparents worrying about the development of their precious grandchild can also offer some fairly stern advice.

As most parents have noticed, there are many experts out there who think they know better than you about how you should raise your child. Amazingly, quite a few of these people don't have children of their own or have even taken care of children. The same applies for bringing up your child to be bilingual. There are those who will warn you of all the perils that are lurking behind the corner should you choose to pass on your languages to your daughter. Again, funnily enough, these people are often not bilinguals, not to mention parents of a bilingual child.

You may also encounter parents of multilingual families where the children have grown up to be either monolingual or passive speakers of one of the family's languages. They might tell you that it will never work and that you may as well give up.

For all these types of situations, arm yourself with the facts about bilinguals and know the myths listed in chapter 4.2 and read on for advice how to handle them.

My partner is not sure bilingualism is right for our family

If this is the situation in your family, and since you are still reading this book and interested in this chapter, I presume you are the parent who would like your child to learn both or all of your family's languages and your partner is not as excited about it. It is very important for the success that you both agree on the strategy, whatever it may be. First, I would recommend that if you haven't already read the section about **Communication**, I suggest you do so now.

You need to find out what lies behind the unwillingness of your partner for your family to choose the multilingual route. Is it the language or are the worries more related to not having a common culture? My guess is that your partner doesn't have anything against the result: your children speaking more than one language. I am sure you have also told your partner about all the advantages there are to be gained. Instead there are most likely other underlying worries, which you need to understand, discuss and come to an agreement about.

The most common reason in situations like this is that one parent is afraid that the child will learn a language that they don't know. The mere thought of your own son saying something that you don't understand can be scary and upsetting. What you need to keep in mind is that he will not learn the language overnight and there are plenty of opportunities for both parents to pick up words along with him - however, the willingness to do so must be present. Both of you also need to agree to speak up if you feel left out of the communication so that something can be done about it. Whatever you do, don't allow the languages to become a bone of contention in the family. To be successful in bringing up your son to be bilingual, you do need to agree about your goals.

The grandparents think it is a bad idea

It is not unusual that grandparents on one side of the family think that you shouldn't teach your daughter your language. In the same way as with a parent, it is rarely the case that grandparents don't want their grandchild to speak more than one language, but rather that there are other concerns behind their reluctance. They may be afraid they will not be able to connect with your daughter if she learns a language they don't know. Perhaps they think that she will not want to stay with them later on in life. Then there are, of course, the sad cases where they never approved of your choice of partner in the first place.

If the latter is true, politely ignore their opinion. They will most likely come round to accepting your multilingual family at one point, so go ahead with your plans. For the other concerns, communication is the key. Find out the real reasons and then dispel the myths and also make sure that you act upon your words, tell them about your daughter's progress and make sure your daughter spends time with them, so they feel that they are not losing out on anything.

If any of your daughter's grandparents think that only one language would suffice, ask them how they would feel if it was their language you decided **not** to teach her. I am sure they would not like it if that was the case.

Discouragement from the family doctor, speech therapist or other professional

One of the most difficult situations a parent of a bilingual child can face is when an expert such as a medical doctor or a speech therapist tells you to only speak one language in the home so not to disadvantage your child. I can't emphasise enough that if this happens to you, always get a second opinion from a doctor or speech therapist who is also familiar with the concept of bilingualism.

Research conducted into different health or speech issues shows that dropping a language is not the solution. On the contrary, changing such an important part in a child's and family's life is more likely to aggravate than alleviate any problems there may be.

If your child has been diagnosed with any form of language or speech development related issue, it does not get worse by the presence of a second language. Someone once compared it to dropping guitar lessons to make it easier to learn to play piano – it doesn't work like that.

Other families have tried and failed

Probably every bilingual person knows a family who has not been successful in passing on their languages to the children. Maybe the children have become passive speakers of the language, which means that they can understand, but can or will not speak it. Perhaps you start thinking, "Well, they are not any different from us, why would we manage it better?" You might even think that since these parents are more highly educated than you are, you have no chance. These parents may advise you not to even try, as it won't work.

Ignore them. The likelihood is that such parents never really thought about how to go about bringing up their children to become bilinguals. Maybe they assumed that it would simply happen and that they would not have to do anything extra to ensure that the languages would be passed on to the next generation. When they noticed that it wasn't happening, the children were in their teens and the parents gave up on the idea.

You might think they are no different from you, but they are. As you are reading this book, you have taken a conscious step to ensure it will not happen in your family. By learning about the different strategies, knowing what is fact and fiction about bilingualism, you are much better prepared to face any hurdles on the way. Keep yourself and your child motivated and you will be successful.

4.3.4 Your child goes to school

Starting school is a major change in a child's life. New surroundings, teachers, new friends, sitting still, following rules – the list of changes and new experiences is endless. Your little boy will be excitedly looking forward to it, but also feeling the butterflies in his stomach. And so will you – not necessarily for the same reasons, but there is a lot to think about. How will he get on? Will he behave? Will he make new friends?

We all want our children to do well at school and in education. We also want to make sure we prepare them for the school and support them the best we can. Secretly we also want them to do better than what we did at school. Maybe you went through school as an "average" student and hope that your son will be among the top achievers. The thought might cross your mind that having to deal with two languages could make it harder for him.

Perhaps you have heard about children being bullied at school because they spoke a different language than the majority. Maybe you are worried that it will take too long for him to catch up with the others as he doesn't yet know the school language. How should you react if your son's teacher claims that his lower than average results are probably due to the home language not being the same as the language spoken at school?

I was never that good at school; won't another language make it more difficult?

Knowing more than one language, no matter which language, gives you an advantage at learning, so it is a benefit rather than a hindrance. Juggling two languages develops certain parts of the brain that are also responsible for concentration and the ability to focus on the relevant pieces of information. This makes bilinguals better at tasks where you have to weed out irrelevant facts. Learning from an early age that everything can have more than one name also widens your son's point of view when confronted with new people and phenomena. Everyone learning more than one language also automatically develops an understanding about language in general, a so-called metalinguistic awareness, which makes it easier to learn more languages.

I've heard that children can get bullied because they talk a different language

Unfortunately, bullying is still a part of school life and language can be one of the things used as an excuse for it. However, the sad truth is, bullies will always find a reason, and dropping a language does not prevent your child from being a victim of it. Always speak with the teachers if you think your son is being bullied at school, no matter what the reason is.

My child does not yet speak the majority language and is starting school

If you have been using the *Minority language at home* strategy to pass on your language to your son and he has not had that much exposure to the majority language before school, he might not yet speak it, or he might only know a little. You might be a new immigrant family and he will start school as soon as you move. Don't worry; being immersed in the majority language through teaching and classmates at school is an extraordinarily effective way for him to pick up the language.

My youngest daughter Daniela was six years old when we moved to England from Finland. She had started speaking rather late, about the age of three and a half, but when we moved, she was fluent both in Swedish and Punjabi. However, she didn't know any English at all. I can't say it didn't worry me; it did – in particular I remember when about a month before our move, Daniela asked me: "Mum, what will I do if I don't understand what the teacher says to me?" It brought tears to my eyes and for a fleeting moment I felt like a bad mother putting her through this ordeal and making her worry at such a young age. I made a promise (which I had no idea if I would be able keep should push come to shove) and said that if she wanted, I would stay with her at school until she felt alright to be there without me. Thankfully, that settled her mind. In Finland, children don't go to school until the age of seven, compared to five in England, which meant she should have started in year two after our move. We asked her to be allowed to start in year one and the school obliged – but it was only needed for a couple of months. It was amazing how quickly Daniela went from knowing no English at all, to starting to understand after about three weeks and beginning to speak her first sentences after three months. I never had to stay with her at school and I needn't have worried. She moved up to year two after a couple of months.

The teacher said our language use delays my child's progress at school

Unfortunately, there are still highly educated teachers who are not aware of how children learn languages in a bilingual setting. If they find that your son is not progressing as expected at school, they might indicate that the reason for it lies in the use of multiple languages – an easy excuse to use. The teacher may even recommend that you stick to the majority language to make sure of your boy's success.

Understandably, we are used to adhering to what authorities such as doctors and teachers tell us. However, in this case you have to stay strong and not give up your language. The additional language is not the reason for lower grades or a slower than expected progress; the cause will be found elsewhere.

If you find yourself having this type of discussion with your son's teacher, make sure to arm yourself with the facts before the meeting, so you can respond to the advice in an appropriate manner. This will allow you to lead the discussion onto the important part: finding out what the actual reason for the slower than expected learning is. Blaming the language will only hide the real reasons and may be damaging for future years.

What to do next?

By now, if you have been reading the book from the start, you should have a good idea of what it means to bring up a bilingual child. You know why you want your daughter to speak more than one language and you have, together with the rest of the family, decided on which strategy is the most suitable for you. You know that the right time to start is now and have an idea about how fluent you want her to become. Hopefully, you have also created your *Family Language Plan*, which you can revisit from time to time to make sure you stay on track.

Being aware of the many myths surrounding bilingualism and how to counter them should have given you confidence in that you have made the right decision. You are also prepared for the more rocky times that may lie ahead: you know how to react if she speaks the "wrong" language to you or when someone questions the wisdom of your plan. You even know how to stand up to professionals that claim you confuse your girl by speaking several languages in the family. All this has strengthened your conviction to go ahead and pass on the family's languages to your daughter.

Now make sure your plans turn into action. You have to commit to your *Family Language Plan* to ensure that your daughter has the best possible chance to grow up acquiring the planned languages. Learning about bilingualism, making the plan and gathering the knowledge to back up your confidence is one thing. Actually doing it is another.

The next section will deal with the practical side of it all, why commitment from the whole family is so important and how to make sure you stay committed to your *Family Language Plan*. What does this commitment mean to you as a family and what should you do when circumstances change and your commitment is put to the test? Let's continue full steam ahead to the next part of our journey: **Commitment**.

"Commitment is what
Transforms the promise into reality.
It is the words that speak
Boldly of your intentions.
And the actions which speak
Louder than the words.
It is making the time
When there is none.
Coming through time
After time after time,
Year after year after year.
Commitment is the stuff
Character is made of;
The power to change
The face of things.
It is the daily triumph
Of integrity over skepticism."

- Ashbash @ urbandictionary.com

5 Commitment

Commitment means that you engage yourself in something you believe in. You make a promise (to yourself and/or others) to act in a certain way and you are willing to invest time and energy into it. It is a fairly big word with life-changing consequences, no matter what the commitment is about – a partner, a career or bringing up a bilingual child.

This section is about defining why it is important to stay committed to your goal. What will your decision mean for you and the whole family? Commitment is an abstract word, but what does it actually entail in your day-to-day lives when you decide to pass on your languages to your son?

Although there are those who pick up their language skills from the family as if by magic, the reality is that these people are fortunate to grow up in an environment where the circumstances are ideal. This is, however, not something that can be taken for granted. To make sure your son does become bilingual, there is an extra bit of effort and awareness required from you. You will need to invest some time and probably also some creativity to make it work. You will have to find ways to offer him the appropriate amount of exposure to the languages he is learning. There are choices you need to make and situations you need to deal with.

Then there's change and how to deal with it. What to do when your family circumstances get altered, for example, if you decide to settle in another country? How should you proceed if your partner is no longer part of the daily life in the same way as before? How will the language balance in the family be affected by the arrival of another child? All these changes can have a major impact on your son's language development. These are situations where your commitment is put to the test, as new circumstances always require more energy, and the choice of language may go down the priority list. Having a firm commitment to your goal will make it easier to stick to your plan or modify it based on the new situation.

5.1 Why is it vital to stay committed to your goal?

There are many factors that influence your decision to bring up a bilingual child. The awareness of the potential advantages will strengthen your determination to succeed. There are also aspects that negatively affect your confidence in your decision. To be able to overcome such hurdles, your commitment needs to stay strong throughout. Having others' support for your goal will make this easier.

Although you and your partner may be speaking different languages to your daughter, it does not mean that she will automatically pick them both up and become an active speaker of them, unless there is enough interactive exposure. It can never be taken for granted that she will acquire the family languages just because she can hear them both spoken every day.

You will have to be engaged in your girl's language learning by providing her with the support she needs at those times when it would be easier to stick to one language. Sometimes you have to be flexible and not insist on her speaking your language – it wouldn't be right to prompt her to use the "right" language if she is in bed with a tummy bug and wants a glass of water. What you do need to do is to go back to using your language when she is well again. Not letting things slip is part of the commitment to your goal. It is good to revisit the *Family Language Plan* from time to time so that your vision of what you want to achieve stays clear in your mind.

As mentioned in chapter 3.3.4, and explained in more detail in the **Consistency** section, you have a vital role in ensuring that your language remains an active language between yourself and your daughter. If you readily switch to the majority language when she happens to answer in the "wrong" language, she will get used to this.

Sooner than you think, the language pattern may change so that your language is only used when there are minority language monolinguals present. A language pattern is not easy to change back and requires much more effort than simply maintaining what you already do.

When you put together your *Family Language Plan*, you wrote down the reasons why you want to bring up your daughter to become bilingual. You also stated the advantages of this decision as well as how fluent you would like her to be. You noted down what it will mean to you and the family to reach your goal. Staying committed to the plan, being engaged and prepared to invest the necessary time and energy will ensure that your vision for the future of the family's language use will come true.

5.2 What does it mean to commit to raising a bilingual child?

It is all very well to say that you are going to do something, writing it down takes a little bit more confidence (I hope your *Family Language Plan* is all complete), but to actually do it is the crucial thing. So what does it mean to commit to bringing up your son to become bilingual?

It will mean that there is one more thing to pay attention to while he is growing up. There is no way around it; it is going to require a bit more effort from you than if you and your family chose to speak majority language of where you are living. You will have to be prepared to invest some of your time to reach your goal. When your son is still learning the language, you need to be ready to have patience and wait while he forms the sentences. You may have to take time out for visits and do the extra bit of reading to increase your son's exposure to the language.

There are also a fair few choices to be made like, for example, what language to speak when others are present. You may have decided on who in the family is speaking what to your boy, but what should

Commitment

you do when monolingual relatives or friends are taking part in the conversation?

For you, it might be an everyday occurrence that a family speaks more than one language, but there are those who will raise an eyebrow at your use of language when out in the public. How will you feel about this? There are also other choices to be made – should you use the family holiday to spend time in the home country or go on the beach holiday you always wanted to experience?

Bringing up your son to become bilingual will undoubtedly have an effect on your family life. I am, however, certain that you can be as successful and have as much fun as a family as you would if you had gone for only one language. Most certainly, you will be extremely delighted with the end result if you persevere.

5.2.1 The little bit of extra effort

Once you have decided that you want to pass on your family's languages to your daughter, be aware that it will require a bit of effort from you, as it will not necessarily happen without you being there to make sure that everyone stays on track.

We have already spoken about situations where your conscious input is needed. You have read about what to do when your boy answers you in the "wrong" language or when your belief in your own abilities seems to weaken. You also know how to respond to those that don't share your belief that raising a bilingual child is a good idea.

In addition there will be situations where you, your daughter or both of you are exhausted by the events of normal everyday life and would prefer to take the easy way out wherever possible. Let's say you had a challenging day at work and pick up your little girl from nursery and she wants to tell you about a game she played with her new friend. You, of course, want to hear about it, but then she describes it all to you in the "wrong" language – should you interrupt her and risk not hearing about it all? No, you shouldn't – listen to her story, no matter what language it is in. Later on in the evening, you may want to pick it up – in your language – and ask about some specifics about what she did. Ensuring that your daughter learns your language shouldn't impact on her wish to share her thoughts with you.

> *I asked my younger daughter about her experiences growing up acquiring three languages. She had mostly positive memories about how happy she felt when relatives were proud of her being able to speak the family's language and others admiring her for being bilingual. There was, however, one thing she did point out to me, which was the frustration she felt when I insisted on her speaking Swedish after her spending a full day at an English-speaking school and having something interesting to tell me at the end of her school day. It seems I was a bit too stringent in my expectation of her using only Swedish when she spoke to me.*

In your *Family Language Plan*, you should also have noted down how you will ensure that your daughter will get enough exposure to both (or all) of your family's languages. This may prove to be easier on paper than in real life. Occasionally check your *Family Language Plan* and do a count in hours to see whether your girl is actually getting as much exposure as you planned. If she isn't, then try to come up with ways to balance the situation.

In the next chapter, you will find advice on how to deal with change in family circumstances – this is where your efforts are needed more than ever.

Commitment

5.2.2 Time investment

Not only does your commitment to raising a bilingual child require extra effort on your behalf, you will also have to invest some of your time in it. Sometimes a few extra seconds or minutes will do – for example, when you wait until your son has found the right word or phrase. You may, on the other hand, notice that an extended time of exposing him to the language is necessary, and you will have to spend some more of your time with him to make it happen.

The need of more time with your son especially applies if you are the minority language parent. Initially, you may find that your son's language exposure tallies up with your *Family Language Plan* and he is easily spending about a third of his waking time in an environment where your language is spoken. This will, however, change when he goes to nursery – in many cases, this is also the point where a parent returns to work, a big change all around in the family.

To ensure that your little boy is continuing to learn more of your language, you will have to put arrangements in place to provide him with enough exposure. Ideally you will do this yourself, by reading to him more, involving him in things you do at home and telling him what you are doing. Remember to use every opportunity for language exposure. Explain what you are doing when gardening, putting up a shelf (an excellent way of learning names of tools), cooking – anything, really.

Watching children's TV programmes is okay, but try to interact with your son while he is doing it by asking questions and pointing things out. If he sits alone and watches and/or listens to TV/DVD/radio programmes/music, it does not compensate for the effectiveness of an engaging chat with him.

If you find that you will not be able to provide enough of exposure for your son, consider asking for help from relatives or friends who can speak your language with him. Maybe they could occasionally pick him up from nursery or school and immerse him in the language. There really doesn't have to be any special activities for this – as long as they don't put him in front of the telly to watch majority language children's programmes!

You may also have to consider how to use your holiday time in the most effective way. If you want to go on a beach holiday, try to find a destination where the minority language is spoken. Spending the time with the extended family, especially with the grandparents, normally turns out to be an effective language immersion method. Maybe you can even take off and have some quality time with your partner while your offspring is being pampered by relatives and learning lots of new words.

5.2.3 Being different as a family

If you have gone for any of the options where you talk more than one language at home (not the *Minority language at home* approach), there will be situations when other people around you will be looking curiously at you. Some people will even wonder out aloud how you can at all communicate when you are not speaking the same language. Again, ignore such comments.

> *We certainly had our fair share of this in our family – especially since we consistently used three languages together. I would speak Swedish with our daughters; the girl's father would speak Finnish with me and Punjabi with the girls. How did we end up with this combination, you may ask. We lived in Finland and it was important that my then-husband learnt Finnish, so that was the language we chose to be our common language when our first daughter Minna was born. At that point, I also spoke Finnish with Minna. We knew from the start that we wanted our children to speak Punjabi, so that they could maintain a good relationship with their father's side of the family in India and England. I have been bilingual since*

childhood (Swedish and Finnish) and it was important for me that our children learnt Swedish, which is a minority language in Finland. Also, I wanted them to attend a Swedish-speaking school. I switched to speaking Swedish with Minna when she was five and our second daughter Daniela learnt Swedish and Punjabi from the outset. We ended up in a situation where we didn't have one common language for all of us. Only Minna knew all three languages, which may seem odd, but it worked for us. Because of the language exposure between ourselves, it also lead to myself getting a moderate passive understanding of Punjabi and Daniela likewise for Finnish.

What is bound to happen is that you find yourself explaining to others how it all works with the languages in your family – again, it is good to be prepared to do some myth-busting during these discussions. My approach to this was to take the opportunity to speak on behalf of all multilingual families and explain what a wonderfully effective way it is to give the children the gift of an additional language for free. Certainly those who have tried to learn a foreign language as an adult will appreciate the value of learning a language as a child.

Being different from the norm always attracts attention, and this may upset children. Children also often want to be "just like everyone else", so you need to keep an eye on your daughter's reactions if the fact that you speak many languages together in public makes her feel uncomfortable. Spending time with other multilingual families is a good way of making your family situation feel "normal" to her. Always make sure that as parents you show your pride for all the family languages as this will influence how she feels about them and how confidently she will use them.

5.2.4 Choices to be made

Deciding to bring up your son to become bilingual also brings with it other choices that you have to make. These might not occur to you straight away, so I am listing some of them here.

Name of your child

I am certainly not going to make any suggestions on what name you should give your son, but I would like you to keep in mind a few things when choosing it. It is a good idea to select a name that is easy to pronounce in both or all of your family's languages. This will prevent the situation that I have heard mentioned by some grandparents who feel a bit uncomfortable with their grandchildren's names being so different from what they are used to: "I can't even pronounce her name." Some families opt to start using nicknames alongside with the given names to circumvent the issue with a "difficult" name.

> *Although 'Minna' is an international name and easy to pronounce in any language, I remember that her Indian grandfather wanted to give her a nickname, so he called her 'Gifty' for a while. However, had we used that name among our Swedish-speaking friends and family members, it would have sounded like the Swedish word 'giftig', which means 'poisonous' – not something you would like to call your child!*

So if you use a name that is more specific to one language than the other, try using it in the other language and make sure there are no unwanted negative connotations with it.

DVDs, TV and other programmes

If you want to watch something as a family, you will need to choose what language the programme will be in. If possible, choose a DVD in the minority language as often as you can – rent or borrow them instead of buying. Switch on the subtitles so that everyone in the family can follow the plot. I know that subtitles take a little effort to get used to, but they are actually an excellent way of picking up words.

> *Minna was an early talker and also learnt to read well when she was about five years old. In the Nordic countries, TV programmes are usually not dubbed but subtitled, so you will be used to hearing different languages in the home. One day when Minna was watching an English TV programme, she made a fleeting comment, which I thought was quite insightful for a five-year-old: "It's easy to learn English, Mummy. You only have to read the text and listen to what they say!"*

Books and magazines

Depending on whether or not you have decided to aim for your son to also be able to read and write in both or all of your family languages, I would still recommend having books and magazines available in all languages. If he can't read them, you can still read them to him. A good idea is to suggest to friends and family that if they plan to give any presents to him, an age-appropriate book would be welcome. Also ask your family to save old magazines for you to use as reading material.

School

Choosing a school for your daughter naturally depends on many different factors, so language can only be one of them. I advise you to find out about the school's attitude to bilingual children in general. Do they support the idea of bilingualism being beneficial, or is the school's support for other than the majority language restricted to one day in the year when they celebrate multiculturalism and everyone brings in typical food items from their culture? It is also useful to find out what the ratio of bilingual children in the school is to get an idea of whether bilingualism is something the school is used to. All this said, the choice of school naturally needs to be based on the best possible education for your daughter – if her language development can be supported by it, all the better. If you are lucky to have a school that offers immersion classes for one of your family languages, then I would recommend you look into that as an option for your little girl.

Hobbies

If at all available, finding hobby groups in the minority language is an excellent way to motivate your son to speak your language. Some communities also arrange weekend or evening school groups which not only teach the language but also are a place for your son to meet other children that speak it. Again, the language shouldn't be the deciding factor here, but if there are hobbies available in your language and your son is interested in them, why not go for this option?

> *When we moved to England, Daniela started attending a Sunday school arranged by the local Sikh temple to improve her Punjabi. She became much more confident in her use of the language and she also learnt to read Punjabi.*

Holidays

Holidays can be an excellent way of immersing your daughter in an environment where your language is the only one spoken. You can still enjoy the type of holiday you like to take, but try to find a place where your language is in the majority. When your daughter is a bit older, she may even go on her own to visit family and friends.

Traditions and celebrations

Multiple languages usually also bring with them different traditions and ways to celebrate various occasions. Which ones you choose to embrace depends, of course, on your own preference, but traditions are a good way to show your pride in your own culture and language. See further in the section on **Culture**.

Choice of language in different situations

This is a choice for which there is no one-size-fits-all answer. Which language you talk in the family and with your daughter when other monolingual friends or relatives are present depends on various other things. This is a topic in its own right, so in chapter 6.4 you will find thoughts about how to deal with different language combination situations.

> *I remember when I travelled to Germany for the first time when I was 19 and wanted to send a postcard to my parents. I had always only spoken Finnish to my mother and Swedish to my father, so it was a bit of a conundrum which language to choose for the card. I didn't want any of them to think the card was only for the other parent (and didn't want to spend money on two cards – I was a student after all), so I wrote the card in alternating Finnish and Swedish words. Apparently my card caused a lot of joy and amusement when it arrived, so it achieved its purpose.*

5.3 How to stick with it when circumstances change

Nothing is as constant in life as change. No matter how much we think we have made the perfect plan and taken all options into consideration, life always throws things at us that we were not expecting. Big changes in family circumstances can upset the balance in many different ways, and language use is no exception to this.

You may have created the perfect *Family Language Plan* and then all of a sudden you find that it can no longer be implemented – should you give up on bringing up a bilingual child? No, you shouldn't. The *Family Language Plan* is meant to be a flexible document that you should modify if the circumstances change.

The joyous occasion of another child in the family can be the reason for a change in the language balance, especially when the siblings start to speak with each other and choose the language for their communication with each other.

Another common situation where a review of the *Family Language Plan* is necessary is if you and your family move to a place where the majority language is different. To ensure that your son continues to get the adequate language exposure, you will have to take stock of the situation.

Then there are the tough situations in a family's life where one parent is no longer as much a part of a child's life. If you are going through difficult times in your life, such as a separation or the passing away of your partner, language use will not be the first thing on your mind, but I will include these situations, as I know these are times when you need advice and support.

What to do if you find a new partner who may not know your son's other language at all? How do you ensure the matter of language use does not negatively affect a situation which is a balancing act at the best of times?

5.3.1 Siblings

The arrival of a new baby in the family can have an effect on the established language setting in a multilingual family. You might think this sounds strange; wouldn't you just continue the same way as you have been doing with the first child? Mostly you certainly will, but there are situations where you may notice that the languages are not used in the same way as before, as the dynamics of the family are different from before. The change will be more significant in a family that follows the *One parent, one language* approach and less so in one that has chosen *Minority language at home* or *Time and place*.

Purely due to the law of availability, you will have less one-to-one time for your second child (and third and so on). You still want to pay attention to your firstborn daughter so that she does not feel left out, but inevitably both your newborn son and your daughter will from now on have less of your time alone with them as you are sharing your time between them. There will be less unique direct interaction between each child and yourself. Since the older sibling(s) will inevitably initially do most of the talking, it is important that you pay attention to also speaking *directly* to your son, so he gets the vital interaction in your language from the outset.

Many families have also noticed that they are less stringent with the language use "rules" in the family with the second child than with the first. This might be due to the fact that they have noticed that it all worked out okay, and are not that concerned about the appropriate amount of exposure of the family languages. However, it is even more important with the second and subsequent children to stick to the *Family Language Plan*.

If your daughter is already at nursery or school when her baby brother is born, she will be more used to speaking the majority language, both with adults and children. She may therefore choose to speak this language with her brother as well. Since the two of them will soon be playing together, the majority language will get more time in your son's life than it got in hers during the first few years. When your children are small, you still have an opportunity to influence their behaviour, so you might want to consider whether you should steer your daughter to choose the minority language as the mode of communication between her and her brother. Later on, no matter what you plan, you will have very little say in what language they speak with each other. What usually happens is that by the time both are at nursery or school, they will be using the majority language between them. However, every bit helps, so do encourage your children to speak the minority language with each other.

Your daughter can also be a great language teacher to her brother, and a far more stringent one than what you would ever be – as many parents have noticed. If you have followed the *One parent, one language* approach, she will probably be the first one to correct her brother if he speaks the "wrong" language with anyone in the family.

In any case, this is again a time when you need to go back to your *Family Language Plan* to check that the new arrival will be getting enough exposure to the minority language. If he doesn't, there is a chance that he only acquires a passive knowledge of the language.

5.3.2 Moving to another country

Moving somewhere where the majority language is different will most likely require you to modify your *Family Language Plan*, but this is okay. The plan was never meant to be set in stone – it has to be adjusted according to the circumstances. The best option is to go through the process of putting together a brand new plan, as there are likely to be changes to more than one aspect of it.

If you have been using the *One parent, one language* approach with both parents speaking their own language and the new majority language is a third language, I would recommend that you continue using the same approach, which means you will become a *Two minority*

Commitment

languages at home family. If you were to drop one of the languages at this point, it would most likely mean that it would become a passive language for your children.

> *We encountered a situation similar to this when we moved from Finland, although we already actually had three languages we used at home: Swedish, Punjabi and Finnish. When we moved to England, another language was added to the mix and we became a 'three minority languages at home' family – and it still worked. Our elder daughter Minna, 13 at the time of the move, had learnt enough English at school in Finland to be able to attend a secondary school in England. Daniela, who was only six, soon picked up the language at school. This also meant that English did sneak into the family so that when we all needed to discuss something together, English was the language of choice for us. At this point, our language set-up was as follows: I spoke Swedish with the girls, their dad spoke Punjabi to them, their dad and I spoke Finnish together. When Daniela learnt English, this became the language we used when we all needed to discuss something together, prior to that, we used a mixture of our languages when speaking together.*

You need to pay special attention to ensure that your son gets enough exposure for both of the minority languages. He will learn the majority language in the nursery, from friends and at school. If you have older children that may feel a bit more self-conscious about not knowing the language, consider tuition outside school, via online resources or a language course. If you want to keep your original languages, then I wouldn't recommend that you change any of the languages you use within the family.

However, if your move means that your *Minority language at home* becomes the majority language, in this case, consider whether it would be viable to change the language you speak at home. These decisions always depend on who can speak what and what feels comfortable to each family member. Any change will feel strange to start with, but if you are committed to maintaining active bilingual skills in the family, consider how much exposure your children get to each language. It is all a question of priorities, but with a little conscious effort and planning, it is possible to ensure that all languages are maintained.

I have seen many families where the parents have both changed to speaking the majority language of the country they have moved to, thinking that this would be the best way to support their children's language learning. The opposite is actually true. In many cases, the parents don't know the majority language that well and don't feel that comfortable in speaking it to their child – this is not an ideal situation at a time when many other changes are happening in a child's life. Also having a strong foundation in the family language is of great advantage when learning the majority language of the society. Children from families which have maintained their home language when moving to a different language environment have been found to learn the majority language more quickly than those coming from families where the parents have adopted the majority language as the common language in the home.

No matter how the language setting changes when you move, review your *Family Language Plan* and revisit it from time to time to stay on track.

5.3.3 Death of a family member

The death of a family member, be it one of the parents or grandparents, is devastating for a family. In a multilingual family, it can also have a great impact on the language setting. Once you have come to terms with the initial shock, you will start to notice that not only have you and your daughter lost a close person, but many other changes have also taken place. The connections the person had with other family members and friends can no longer be taken for granted. Your daughter may have lost not only a person she loved, but she might no longer have as much support for her languages.

Every family experiences the loss of a family member differently and there are no hard and fast recommendations on how to compensate for the language support. If the person was the only one who spoke one of the family languages with your daughter, it could take time before the language can be reintroduced. In such a case and when it feels right, try to create some new positive memories associated with the language. Ask other relatives and friends to get more involved so your daughter can get enough exposure to the language again. The language was a big part of the family life before and the person who passed away would have wanted the language to continue to be an active part of it.

Which language to use is not the first thing on your mind when you are grieving, but once you feel that you can look forward again, give the *Family Language Plan* a thought and revise it.

5.3.4 Divorce or separation

When parents separate, it is a tragedy for the children, no matter what their age. In a multilingual family, a separation can lead to big losses on many levels for the children. In the "ideal" situation, the split is amicable and the parents manage to keep in mind what is best for the children. The children will still be spending time with both parents and both sides of the family, so with regards to the language exposure, there might still be enough of it in the new circumstances.

Unfortunately, far too few separations go that well and there are a lot of negative emotions and the children get drawn into disagreements between their parents. For the children, a divorce might lead to less contact with one of the parents and that parent's side of the family. If the parent is the minority language parent, there is a risk that the children stop speaking the language as well. What to do? Should you support keeping up the language skills although you would rather not? In my opinion, yes, if at all possible.

I know a separation is upsetting and can cause resentment, but try to look at it from the children's angle and not transfer your emotions for the person and the language onto your children. Even in the sad scenario where they may lose contact with the other parent's side of the family for now, think about what will happen in the future. The likelihood is that they would like to stay in contact with their relatives when they grow up. A common language would make this so much easier, and also more likely to happen. After all, the children weren't the ones to decide about the separation.

If you find yourself in a situation where the amount of contact with the other side of the family is significantly reduced, take a deep breath and revisit the *Family Language Plan*. Think of other ways to support your children's language development. Of course, you have to take into account the age of the children – if any of them haven't started talking yet, you will have to be prepared to put in some effort to continue supporting the minority language.

5.3.5 New family with a step-parent

Another situation where you will have to review your *Family Language Plan* is the happy occasion of a new family being created by combining two existing ones. Although the occasion is a joyous one, it also takes a lot of adjusting on all sides, not least by the children.

If the new family combination also means a different language set-up, then the best thing to do is to create a completely new *Family Language Plan*. Sit down with everyone in the family and go through the whys, whats, whos, whens and hows of the plan, letting everyone have their say.

If a child loses the support of a minority language through the new family arrangement, then you need to pay special attention to this part. How will you ensure that the language stays active in the child's life? What additional resources do you need and who are the people that can support you?

105

For a newly formed family, a common language is important, as bonding and creating a family unit is most likely one of the greater challenges in these situations. You wouldn't want to add to this challenge through the use of your languages. This, however, shouldn't mean that you give up on the language which you are used to speaking with your children from the previous relationship. Your children are experiencing enough new things in their lives without another major change which the drop of your old common language would inevitably be.

What to do if your new partner (and possibly your children's new siblings) don't understand your common language at all? There are no simple answers to this, as it depends on the relationships within the family. In any case, try to avoid situations where you might be perceived to use a "secret" language in front of other family members that don't understand what you are saying. It is not that you are trying to keep something hidden, but others may feel like you do. This is something that we bilingual people sometimes forget – the feeling of being left out if you don't understand a language. It is not something we are that used to.

Make time for situations where everyone can freely speak their preferred languages without anyone feeling excluded. This will need a bit of planning but it is well worth it, not only for the language support, but also for bonding. The more languages you have in the family, the more conscious effort you will have to put in to support them.

What next?

So we have sailed through the first three Cs of bringing up a multilingual child: **Communication**, **Confidence** and **Commitment**. So far, it has been more about the theory than the practice of a multilingual family. You have thought about and discussed it; you have gathered the facts and picked up confidence. Finally, you have committed to your *Family Language Plan* – what next?

In the next section, we will go into more of the nitty-gritty of the everyday life of a family where more than one language is spoken by the parents and children. This is important whether you have chosen the *One parent, one language, Minority language at home* or *Time and place* strategy to pass on the family languages to the next generation.

Any parenting guide will tell you that consistency is a vital part of parenting, be it in any circumstance. Being consistent in your behaviour creates stability and safety for your son; he knows what will happen. It also serves to set the all-important boundaries for the desired behaviour.

To achieve your goal of bilingual offspring, aim at as much consistency as you can. This applies to who speaks what language when, what to speak when others are around and how to ensure the quality of the language your son gets exposed to. There are also some things that you should be doing and others that should be left undone to support your son in the best possible way.

In the midst of being consistent with this, that and the other, don't forget that your son's well-being comes first. Don't let the idea of being consistent make you rigid and inflexible in your behaviour. I trust you will use your common sense when you notice that a situation needs a more open approach in order to avoid a tantrum, conflict, misunderstanding or whatever life may throw at you. Let's continue our journey to the next C: **Consistency**.

Commitment

*"Success is more a function
of consistent common sense
than it is of genius."*

- An Wang

6 Consistency

The word 'consistent' can be defined as having a steady continuity, regularity and harmony. Something that is consistent is also free from contradiction. Those are all wonderful words for your parenting journey, aren't they? To grow up to become a balanced adult, you ideally want those qualities around you as a child. In the same way, consistency is what your daughter needs to pick up both or all of your family languages and to use them without effort in her everyday life.

In this section, I will go into more detail about why consistency is important when bringing up a bilingual child. Note that I am not saying that bilingual children can only be raised in families that are consistent about their language use. What I do think though is that the probability that your daughter will be confidently communicating in the family languages is higher if there is a level of consistency in her exposure to them while she is growing up.

I will also go into the importance of the quality of communication and how to make sure that your girl has good role models for her language. Remember that even if you feel that you might not speak your language perfectly, you can still bring up your daughter to speak your language. You do, however, have to make sure there is enough language input from other speakers as well.

There will be occasions where the consistency of your language use is put to the test. What to do when there are other children or adults around you that don't understand the language you normally speak with your daughter. Should you stick with it or switch to a common language?

In order to be consistent, there are some things you should do and others which you shouldn't. This is absolutely correct. Although being consistent doesn't mean being inflexible, there are certain things that you may not even think about which are a no-no when raising your daughter to become bilingual. Then again, there are some aspects that should be part of your everyday routine and which will be extremely beneficial for her language development.

6.1 Consistent use of language at home

I love the quote from An Wang at the start of this section:

"Success is more a function of consistent common sense than it is of genius."

Nothing could be truer when bringing up a bilingual child. You don't need to be a linguistic talent or highly educated to be able to successfully raise your son to become a bilingual. To give your family the best possible chance of succeeding, it is, however, best to stay consistent in your language use with him. When implementing consistent language patterns within the family, you strengthen the minority language's position in the communication structure. The minority language runs the risk of losing impetus if it regularly loses out when children want to speak the language they have been using all day at school, and a parent or the whole family switches to the majority language.

The rule of consistency applies independently of whether you have opted for *One parent, One language*, *Minority language at home* or *Time and place* strategy. With the mixed use approach, there are no real rules so the principle is not relevant.

One parent, one language

The *One parent, one language* method is straightforward with regards to being consistent: one parent uses one language with the children, the other parent another language. If both parents understand the other language, the language setting is fairly easy to implement.

Every *One parent, one language* family will, however, have to decide which language to use when the whole family is together. In cases where everybody can communicate in the minority language, it is recommended to choose this as the common language of the family to increase the amount of exposure to it. If the only language that both parents can speak is the majority language, then of course, this will also end up being the language the family speaks when everyone is taking part in a discussion.

When each parent (or even a grandparent or childminder, providing they spend enough time with the child) speaks a different language, the child quickly establishes a pattern for what to speak with each person and the choice of language becomes second nature.

Consistency combined with enough exposure will make it possible even for one parent to pass on the language without much support from other sources. I know that some experts in the field have stated that this is not possible, but our family is proof of the opposite.

My daughters' father was more or less the only person speaking Punjabi to Minna and Daniela prior to us moving to England. When we lived in Finland, none of their father's side of the family lived close and there were only a few other Punjabi-speaking families that we occasionally met up with. This meant that they had little interaction in Punjabi other than with their father. We had the odd video and music cassettes in Punjabi, but that was it. At the time of the move, Minna was thirteen and Daniela six years old and they were both able to confidently communicate in Punjabi. Their grammar was not perfect and vocabulary might have been a bit restricted, but they spoke the language without hesitation. To my surprise, this was often not the case with children of Punjabi families in England. I noticed that the major difference between our family and others were that we had always been consistent in our language use. Their father had always spoken only Punjabi to them, whereas many parents we knew in England

Consistency

had swapped between English and Punjabi when speaking to their children.

Minority language at home

With the *Minority language at home* approach, it should be even easier to stay consistent: the only language the parents speak with the children is the minority language. I say 'should' as it doesn't always turn out to be that straightforward. This might be because the choice to speak the lesser used language is not always a conscious one; it is often something that just happens. Maybe the parents spoke the minority language together before the children were born and so it was a given that it would also be the common language with the children.

So why don't all children in families where the parents initially only spoke a minority language become active speakers of their parents' native language? The family language pattern can easily change at the point where the children spend more time at school and with their majority language friends. The majority language makes its entrance into the home and if parents are not conscious of this shift, the majority language may oust the minority language as the common language of the family.

How persistent should you be? As always, do stay persistent in that the main language at home should still be the minority language, but don't allow it to become a major area of contention. When your son wants to tell you how he scored his first goal in the school football team, let him do it in the language he wants.

The one thing that you will most likely not have any say in is what your son and daughter speak when they are together. The likelihood is that it will be whatever language they use at school, as they will have more interaction in that language as they grow older. Although you can't change the language they speak with each other, what you can do is to gently insist on the minority language staying the common language when the family is together.

Time and place

If you have opted for the *Time and place* strategy, then consistency should be at the forefront of your mind at all times when communicating with your daughter. It is important that you stick to whatever plan you have made, be it speaking language A every other week and language B in-between, or A in the living room and B everywhere else at home.

If you have chosen, for example, the weekends and Wednesdays to be the time when you speak language A with her, then put in place family routines to support this. Arrange activities where you can practise the language and use it in your natural communication.

If your preferred option is to speak language A in a specific room at home, then choose a room where you spend time regularly during the day. I know it may sound strange to change language when moving from one room to another, but it has been proven to work – you do have to stay very consistent though.

Another option for this approach is to pick certain activities during which you always speak a certain language. Again, if you do this, you need to make sure that the activities you choose are ones that you do often enough and during which you actively communicate.

Use lots of supporting material if you decide to go down the *Time and place* route. Have books, magazines and DVDs that you can enjoy together, especially for the minority language.

6.2 The DOs and the DO NOTs

The very quality of being consistent means that there are some things you do over and over again and others that you avoid. Like anything else with parenting, there will be some situations where you will have to make exceptions, but the behaviours described in this chapter can be used as a guideline for what the ideal situation would look

Consistency

like. This said, each of the always-DOs and the absolute-DO-NOTs are ones that I recommend you take to heart. Some of them are blatantly obvious and should be part of any parent's behaviour, but they still need to be brought up, so bear with me. If you are already doing/not doing these, then give yourself a pat on the back and reward yourself with something nice.

The always-DOs

Praise

We all know how good it feels inside when someone tells us we've done something well. Strangely, we don't remember to tell others often enough when we think they have succeeded in something. Children thrive in an environment with a lot of positive feedback. I don't, however, mean to go overboard as in, "Well done for breaking only one flowerpot!" but giving genuine praise where it is called for – children are extremely good at detecting if you are being honest. To support your son's language learning, make praise a part of your life. When he expresses himself well in your language, recognise it. Note new words he uses in your *Language Success Diary*. Write down the funny phrases and stories he tells. Read about the *Language Success Diary* and positive feedback in the **Celebration** section.

Have patience

I can't emphasise enough how important it is for you to be patient when your son is learning to speak your language. Even if you are in a hurry, don't rush him or immediately offer words that he can't find right away. On the other hand, if he asks what things are called in your language, answer every time. On those occasions where you don't know the name for something (who knows all the bird and flower names in their native language?), take the opportunity to look up the word later. Maybe keep a small notebook where you write down words you need to investigate so you don't forget. Don't feel bad if you don't know all words, no one does. Showing patience signals to your son that it is okay for him to think while he is talking, and that there is no pressure. Also have patience when you notice that he might be using an incorrect word; don't jump in and correct (see about correcting later in the section). Instead, rephrase what he said in a correct way. Be patient – the more time you give him, the more he will impress you.

Be proud

Show your pride in your own language – your attitude to it will affect how your son feels about it. If you don't feel proud of your language, take a deep look at why this is. Has someone said something that has affected your feelings about your language? Have you had bad experiences in connection with the language? If any of those are true, think it through and find the real reason why you don't feel as positive about your language as you should. You have every reason and right to be proud of the language you speak and you can pass on the same attitude to your son as well. Being proud of all the languages he speaks will make your boy keen on using them whenever he can.

Be persistent

Closely linked to being patient, being persistent in working towards your goal of passing on your language to your son is an important part of your commitment to your *Family Language Plan*. Again, I don't want you to take your persistence to the extreme so that it makes him feel uncomfortable. What you *should* do, however, is to show how important the language is to you and that you will gently insist on him speaking the language with you. He should be aware that even if you on the odd occasion switch to another language, you will always go back to using your language with him. If you switch too readily, he might at some point continue speaking the majority language with you.

Consistency

The try to DOs

Have fun

Try to associate learning and speaking your language with fun things as much as you can: games, word play, stories, celebrations, family fun days, anything you can think of that your daughter enjoys. The more positive associations she has with the language, the more likely she is to keep it up in her life and also pass it on to her children. I know that everyday life might not always feel like fun, but do make the extra effort to create those special moments in your use of language with her. Read more about having fun in the sections about **Creativity** and **Celebration**.

Motivate

You know it from yourself: if you feel motivated to do something, the likelihood that you will actually do it is a hundredfold greater. The same goes for your daughter and her language learning. Find out what positive motivation you can create for her to speak your language. Note the emphasis on the word 'positive' – I firmly believe that carrots work better than sticks. Closely related to the previous behaviour, it is all about creating a good feeling about the language. As your daughter grows, the ways to motivate her will, of course, change. Remember that "rewards" don't have to mean a financial expenditure for you. Take her to the playground, bake a cake or invite her friends around. See the **Creativity** section for more ideas.

Be practical

There are things that you should and shouldn't do, but remember to keep it practical. Sometimes you can't stick to the "rules". If your daughter wants to sing a song with you in the majority language, go along with it. It is probably an indication that she likes singing and you might want to find some songs you can share in your language. If you have had a challenging day at work and she wants help with her school homework, which is in the majority language, do so without necessarily trying to translate everything. There is no need to make things harder than they are – a successful outcome is the crucial thing.

Repeat, rephrase, reread

"Repetition is the mother of learning" is probably a quote you have heard before, and it also applies to language learning. It is useful for your daughter to hear new words and phrases several times in different contexts – so say it again. If your daughter uses a word incorrectly, rephrase what she said so that she can hear the correct version. Last but not least: when she asks you to read the same story for the umpteenth time, do it. I know it can feel tedious but research has shown that it helps her to learn any new words in the story better than if the new words appeared in different stories.

The preferable DO NOTs

Don't be rigid

Although there are rules to be followed to be successful at raising a bilingual child, don't let these principles become so rigid that it takes the fun out of learning and speaking your language. As always with children, you need to be flexible and go with the flow when the situation calls for it. You want your son's use of your language to be something he enjoys; it shouldn't become a chore or something he avoids because of the negative associations with it.

Don't expect perfection

Of course, we all dream that our children will grow up and acquire a perfect command of whatever language we pass on. In reality, this is, however, rarely the case. Depending on the amount of exposure and the availability of opportunities to use a language, the fluency attained will vary greatly. If at any point you worry about your son not speaking your language as fluently as you would like him to, think

Consistency

about what is important. What were the reasons you wanted him to be able to speak your language? Can he communicate with his grandparents and relatives? Is he happy to use the language in his everyday life? If he does, then a few grammar errors here and there, some word pronounced slightly differently or an accent aren't really anything to worry about.

Don't constantly correct

It is alright to offer the correct version by rephrasing what your son said. Don't, however, make this a habit so that you always give the right word or pronunciation when there is something he says that is not quite right. If he is always corrected in what he says, your son might lose confidence in his own ability to speak or learn the language. Being frequently "put right" might negatively affect his motivation to learn more.

The absolute DO NOTs

Don't criticise

Never criticise your daughter's language use. You might at times want to comment on which language or word she uses in a particular situation, how she pronounces a word or any other aspect of her communication – the advice is the same, don't criticise. If you feel the need to recommend another way of saying something, repeat what she said in the way you think is correct/better/more appropriate. You could also try making a comment such as, "Did you mean to say...?" or "I didn't quite catch that ..."

Don't compare

Comparing any aspect of your daughter's progress with other children is not helpful. Children are different and develop and learn at a different pace. Don't compare her to her siblings or any other children. It makes me sad when I hear parents commenting on their children's language skills along the way of, "She hasn't learnt the language as well as her cousin," or, "The neighbour's kids can speak much more fluently than you do." If you are truly worried about your daughter's communication skills (in any language), speak to a specialist; don't pass your own verdict. If you do consult a specialist, make sure to choose one that has experience in dealing with bilinguals.

Don't expect her to "perform"

No matter how proud you are about what languages your daughter knows – don't ask her to say something in front of others to prove she can. I would even recommend diffusing situations where another adult asks your little girl to speak to show she knows a language. The result is usually a refusal to speak at all. In such a situation, your daughter may not even want to respond to *you* even though you would normally speak the language with each other. Languages should be a normal part of her life, not something she has to show off or be nervous about. Children can be sensitive about their language skills and afraid of making mistakes. If, in addition, they are also of a shy nature, asking them to utter something in a particular language for the sake of it is not the right thing to do. Languages should be used in natural situations.

Don't demand

This is, for me, a given, but needs to be noted. You want your daughter to speak your language, but trying to force her to do it is not the way to achieve your goal. By all means, make learning your language *compelling* for her by creating an environment which is motivating and supporting for her development, but don't try to make her do it.

Consistency

6.3 Quantity and quality of communication

With any learning process, the result depends on how much tuition you get and the quality of the tuition. The same goes for your son learning to speak your language. You need to ensure that he gets enough exposure to it and that enough of the exposure is of a good quality.

Rest assured, however, that I don't mean that you have to be able to master the language perfectly – I have touched on this before and I will expand on it in this section. You will need to make sure that your son spends time with other speakers of your language as well. With "good quality language", I don't mean perfect, faultless, spoken-as-written or academic language, but language spoken by a fluent speaker of your language.

There are also certain things that you need to be aware of that are not as effective as you might first think when it comes to arranging quality language exposure for your son. Watching DVDs or TV programmes isn't enough, I am afraid.

For your son to learn your family's languages, he should ideally be exposed to them about 30% of his waking time. Drawing up your *Family Language Plan* will give you the facts about the current situation and will allow you to take the necessary measures to ensure that your son gets enough exposure for the languages he is learning.

Quantity

Experts agree that for children to naturally acquire an additional language, they should ideally be exposed to the language for 30% of their waking time. This is the amount to aim for when your daughter is growing up learning your language. If she sleeps about nine hours over a 24 hour period, it leaves you with 15 hours of waking time, which means she should be exposed to the language for about five hours. This should be counted as an average over a week or two, so it doesn't matter if you don't quite reach the five hours every day of the week, as long as you make up for it during the weekend. All this said, I know that you can bring up a bilingual child with less than 30% exposure to a language – as this has certainly been the case in my family.

When you calculate how much exposure your daughter is getting, be careful how you record it. For example, her being at home with other family members who speak the language with each other doesn't necessarily mean she is actively exposed to the language. If she watches TV programmes in the majority language or plays by herself, she isn't getting the exposure. Therefore, it is important that there is as much interaction as possible.

Make it a habit to speak with your daughter in your language from the moment you know she will be in your life. If you get used to the habit early on, it will come naturally to you at the point where it is important that you speak with her a lot. I know that telling a "bump" about your day may come easier to mums than to dads, but it is equally important. When she is a baby, speak out loud when you are with her – talk about anything: explain what you are doing, plan your shopping list aloud or describe how you are bleeding the radiators. It is not that important what you say, as long as you speak your language and engage her in your discussion. Sooner than you can imagine, she will start communicating and mimicking your behaviour. What a wonderful feeling!

Consistency

Keep your *Family Language Plan* in mind at all times and go back to review it a few times a year while your daughter is small to be sure you are still on the right track. Remember that the 30% minimum recommendation applies to the language that is in the minority in the society you live in. Don't worry if your daughter is exposed to the minority language almost all of the time during her first years. She will still learn the majority language when she goes to nursery or school.

I can't emphasise enough how important it is to boost the amount of time your daughter is exposed to the minority language. If you notice the real exposure time getting much less than 20%, try to find ways to boost it. Whenever possible, overdo the exposure to the minority language during the years before she goes to nursery or school. It will give her a solid start for her bilingual future. From the day she starts nursery (presuming it is in the majority language), her skills in the majority language will keep growing at a fast pace. Unless you keep up the amount of minority language exposure, it might lose out and you'll find one day that she answers you in the "wrong" language. She can't get too much of the minority language exposure, so maximise it as best as you can.

In a *One parent, one language* family, it is a good idea for the minority language parent to increase the one-to-one time with the child at the point where more and more of the majority language is creeping in to the discussions at home. This is a crucial stage of your daughter's language development and if you leave it completely up to her to choose the language she speaks at home, it is highly likely that she goes for the majority language. Be persistent and use the minority language in the same way as you have done up to now – she will change back to responding in the "right" language when you show that you will not change your language use. After all, she is bilingual and every bilingual has a natural tendency to want to use the same language as the other person.

Quality

What does "quality" mean when referring to a spoken language? This is a difficult question, and the answer will always be subjective. In the context of this book, by good "quality" I mean language which is spoken by someone who is fluent in it. The speaker doesn't have to be highly educated, professional or especially well spoken.

Seek the company of native speakers to boost the time your son is exposed to your language. They can naturally be found in the extended family and among friends, but don't forget playgroups, hobbies and children's sports and other activities. Combining something that your son loves with being immersed in the language is the ideal environment for his language learning. If you can't find these in the country you are living in, look for holiday or summer camps. If these are not viable alternatives, consider letting him spend time with the extended family on his own. I know you would probably want to accompany him, but he will learn more effectively if you are not there to jump in and translate.

I do find it a bit unnerving to write about the "quality" of language. The reason is that I don't want you to think that your way of speaking might not be good enough – it is. Full stop. The fact that you might think you don't have an extensive vocabulary or sometimes get a grammatical form incorrect means nothing compared with all the other things you do to support your son's language development. You are the positive role model that he needs to grow up to want to speak your language. By showing that you are proud of your language and culture, you will pass this feeling on to your boy and it will make his language learning more effective.

If you want to expose him to a wide vocabulary, then look no further than to children's books. They are a vast, excellent source of entertainment and education. Not to mention how much he will appreciate the time you spend with him reading a good book. When it comes to books, I can't emphasise enough how important it is that you read bedtime stories to your boy. Giving him the gift of loving books and wanting to learn to read will do so much for his language. Moreover, you will actually expand your own vocabulary as well by reading aloud to him. In a *One parent, one language* family, it is especially important that the minority language parent reads the bedtime stories as often as possible. Why not record some stories as well to have them at the ready when the minority language parent is unable to be there at bedtime?

Many children's programmes also contain excellent language and can be used to supplement the language exposure. However, remember that unless you can make the watching experience interactive in some way, it will not have that much of an impact on your son's learning. Human interaction is crucial in the learning process and no matter how many DVDs or TV programmes your boy gets to watch, they are no match for real life story telling.

6.4 What to speak when others are around

So you have it all set in your family – you know who should speak what to whom in everyday situations. You have a routine that works for you and you are comfortable with it. So what should you do when you are outside the home, in an environment where most of the people speak a different language to the one you do?

Also, what should you do when someone else enters your ideal language set-up and the dynamics change? Should you rigorously stick to what you are used to, or should you change your language use as soon as someone else joins the conversation?

Family outside the home

I don't think that you should change your language use when you are out and about as a family, unless it is required to make yourself understood, of course, or if you have a strong feeling of it being impolite to speak a language other people don't understand.

It is important that your daughter gets used to speaking your language also outside the familiar home environment. Your language shouldn't become a curiosity only used within the family and in your house. It should be the natural means of communication wherever you are. This does mean that in certain societies you might be the one different family among several others, but don't let this hold you back – proudly be the family you are.

Don't take me wrong here – I am not saying that, for example, immigrant families should always keep to their language, and in some extreme cases not even learn the language of the society they are living in. I definitely believe in integrating into the life of the new country and also learning its language, but this does not have to mean that you lose your own cultural and language identity.

When you speak a different language from the majority, keep in mind that there is a common tendency among people that don't understand a language to think that you speak about them. If you, for example, happen to look at them and then say something in your language to someone in your company and laugh, the person you looked at might think you are laughing about them. A bit of caution is to be recommended, to avoid being misunderstood.

On the other hand, it is quite fun to have your own "secret" language when you are out as a family. However, don't forget that there can be people around that do understand what you are saying, even though they don't look like they would.

I have experienced these kinds of situations a few times – from both sides – and they can be quite funny and potentially embarrassing. Once when I went to a shop (in London) with my ex-husband, I commented on the high price of a piece of clothing in Finnish to which the shop assistant responded in clear Finnish that "the quality is, however, top notch". Another time, I stood next to an Asian couple speaking Punjabi and they were complaining that the street signs were unclear and

Consistency

they didn't know how to find their way to the train station. Imagine their surprise when I turned around and explained to them in my very basic but somewhat understandable Punjabi which way they should take (luckily, they weren't too far away from their destination).

Guests in the home

Again, there is no simple answer to this question – your choice of language depends on many factors: whether the others also understand all the spoken languages or whether there are monolinguals present. The age of the other people will make a difference as well as how comfortable you feel in the company. As long as the communication flows and no one feels left out, there is no right or wrong approach.

The general rule is to favour the minority language unless there is someone present who doesn't have any, even passive knowledge of the language. In a group of active and passive bilinguals – with your children present – try to stick to the minority language as much as possible, but make it clear that anyone can speak the language they feel most comfortable with.

My mother came from a monolingual Finnish family from a village where only Finnish was spoken. She had little exposure to Swedish before she met my father. My father, on the other hand, came from a purely Swedish-speaking family, but he had learnt some Finnish as a child when he was playing with the children of a Finnish-speaking family. Furthermore, his home village had both Finnish and Swedish speakers. Therefore, my parents' common language was Finnish. My mother did come in contact with many monolingual Swedish speakers, but I hardly ever heard her speak Swedish, although she understood it well. What she would do was to answer in Finnish when someone spoke to her and the conversation flowed well.

To an outsider, it may sound odd when two people communicate using different languages, but as long as both (or all) parties are fine with it and understand what the others say, there is no reason why people shouldn't communicate this way.

The best thing for your daughter (especially if she is still learning the language) is not to change your behaviour with regards to which language you speak directly to her – even when you are in a company where nobody else understands what you say. If you notice that someone is uncomfortable with the situation, make it a habit to repeat what you said but direct it more to others than to her – you'll know what to do if the situation arises.

Remember to always be sensitive about how your daughter feels about the situation – if she thinks it is awkward that you speak a different language to her when others are around, then don't do it. During a certain stage in their life, children tend to feel embarrassed about their parents, so don't make it worse by putting her in a situation where she thinks you are behaving in a way that makes her feel uneasy.

What next?

Consistency is important when bringing up a child and even more so with regards to passing on your language. Hopefully, this section has given you some ideas on how to maintain the consistency in your family's language use in order to give your son the best start with his language development. Try to keep those DOs and DO NOTs in mind; maybe reread the **Consistency** section now and then so you don't get into any bad habits and so that you keep on encouraging your son in the right way.

If you have read my book from the start, by now you know about four of the seven Cs which multilingual parents have to navigate: **Communication**, **Confidence**, **Commitment** and **Consistency**. What else do you need to consider to ensure that your son grows up to live and love the life of a bilingual?

Well, sometimes multilingual families hit rough seas and maybe even go off course for a while. When this happens, or if you want to do something different, a bit of **Creativity** can give you the boost you need to get some wind in your sails again. In the next section, you will find out about how to use your own creativity (oh yes, you are creative as well!) to make the language learning process easier and more fun.

7 Creativity

There are no off-the-shelf solutions for all the challenges a multilingual family can come across. For these situations, you need to tap into your creativity and use it as a tool to achieve the goals you have defined in your *Family Language Plan*.

If you think you are not creative, let me inform you that you are wrong. Everyone has a creative streak in them – the main thing is to silence one's inner critic and just let it happen. Creativity doesn't mean that you have to come up with a masterpiece in music, art or literature. You don't even have to know how to draw or how to structure a story, but I can assure you, if you give it a go, you will end up with both a drawing and a story which you and your daughter can both be proud of and which will help your daughter in her language uptake.

There are certain situations where it is necessary for you to think on your feet and come up with solutions so that your girl stays on track with her language development. All sorts of challenges can crop up and I will give a few examples on ways to use creativity to overcome such obstacles.

Remember that there are plenty of resources out there to help you in your quest to raise your daughter to be bilingual. First, of course, there are the members of the extended family who can come to your rescue when you don't know what to do. Other multilingual families would be happy to share their experiences and insights with you. There is also a lot of advice available online and through other media – visit www.multilingualparenting.com to find ideas and advice, and to connect with other multilingual families.

Creativity

*"Creativity is a great motivator
because it makes people interested
in what they are doing.*

*Creativity gives hope
that there can be a worthwhile idea.*

*Creativity gives the possibility of
some sort of achievement to everyone.*

*Creativity makes life
more fun and more interesting."*

- Edward de Bono

7.1 How you can be creative

Creativity is not something only artists, musicians, painters and writers have – we all have it within us, but we might not ever have been encouraged to use it. This again might lead us to think that we aren't creative. Wrong! Letting go of the perception that creativity is a rare and extraordinary commodity and instead looking around you for inspiration, will allow you to come up with new ideas.

To allow creativity into your everyday life, start with what you already know. Think back to your childhood and what you did with your friends – could this be something you could do with your son? If you don't remember, ask others – your parents or even grandparents, if you are fortunate to still have them around.

Nothing is as creative as a child's mind. You only need to start something and your son will pick it up. There are no restrictions as to what can be done and what could happen – let him lead you, and sooner than you know, you will come up with something exciting together.

Keeping it simple will make the task less daunting – you don't need expensive equipment. Make a castle out of a cardboard box and change it to a super fast car if your son wants to – all the time describing what you do and asking questions so that he can expand his vocabulary.

7.1.1 Start with what you know

Let's say you want to come up with a game that you can play with your daughter so you can have fun together and practise your language at the same time. You might think, "I wouldn't know where to start!" Well, start with what you know. What games did you play with your siblings or friends when you were small? Could you play the same game with your daughter, maybe adjusting it a bit to suit where you are or what you have available? Ask your daughter, let her suggest what you could do, and hey presto, you have come up with a game you can play together.

Creativity

If you can't remember what you used to play, ask your parents or grandparents or speak to your childhood friends. How exciting would that be to hook up with them again and chat about old times – what a bonus! Your parents and grandparents would be delighted to tell you what they did when they were small. Your daughter might be keener than you think on making something out of matchsticks and potatoes. If not, it sure does make a good story that you can pass on to her.

When it comes to stories, you don't have to make them up. Tell your daughter about what you were interested in as a child, what you experienced and what happened to you. Your life is an endless supply of stories that you can pass on, not to mention the tales that the older generation can contribute. With these, not only do you have a treasure chest of stories, but you are passing on family history and traditions when you tell them as bedtime stories. If you record them, your daughter can listen to them again and again whenever she wants.

If you have moved away from your home country, why not create a space in your home that reminds you of it? It can be the place where you sit with your daughter and tell family stories. I do realise that this is not going to happen any longer when she is a teenager, but cherish the time when she still wants to do it. When she is older, the space will bring back happy memories for her.

7.1.2 Let your child lead you

If you have any doubts about your own ability to come up with stories, games or ways to solve things, there is someone close to you that has no such inhibitions: your son. As are all children, he is brilliant at coming up with characters, plots and different ways of doing things.

When you want to come up with new ways of engaging with your boy which are conducive to him learning your language, more often than not the only thing you need to do is either start a story or a picture, bring out a toy or draw on what he is interested in. You can introduce new words and phrases by weaving them into your story, drawing or play. By using the new words and phrases in an interesting context, your son will pick them up quicker than you think.

Start a story

A child's imagination has no limits – you will notice this if you sit down with your boy and start with "Once upon a time, there was a ..." and let him complete the sentence. Trust me, he will come up with something. From then on, it is easy for you – move the story on by asking question such as: I wonder what the striped rabbit did? What happened to him? Who were his friends? What did they do? Why did he do that? Where did he live? What did he eat? What did he wish for? What was he good at?

In case you want to take the story towards something specific, add a character or a situation or anything you want. If you would like your son to learn vegetable names, make the rabbit taste them. If animals are the topic of the day, let the rabbit meet them all (and have fun making all the animal noises).

A great way to start a story is to make it about your son: "Once, there was a little boy called [your son's name] and he ..." – you'll be surprised with what the story might turn into. Making up stories together is a great way to bond and it will give him many memorable moments.

Since most mobile phones now have voice recorders on them, why not record your unique stories? When you get the time, you could even write them down and make them into a book. I know this takes time, so remember to store the files in a safe place somewhere for later. But wouldn't it be great to have your own books to pass on to your daughter and the next generation?

Creativity

Draw a picture

If your son is more visual and captivated by pictures, create a drawing and make a story out of it. "But I can't draw", I hear you say. Honestly, you can draw stick people and you can draw a rabbit: a small circle on top of a bigger one, two ears, a pair of eyes and a nose, then add the paws and you've got a rabbit! If it needs to be striped, that's easy to do. Then you can turn the picture into a story with the help of your son.

What you think are simple scribbles, in his mind your son can turn them into an exciting adventure. Take it in turns and add something to your picture – again, if you want to teach your little boy some new words, include them in it. If you feel uncomfortable in drawing yourself, cut something from a magazine to start with and let your son add to it.

Put your picture on the wall, where you can look at it together and repeat the new words that you included in it. When you don't have space for any more pictures on your kitchen wall, save them in a folder which becomes your own picture storybook. Always put a date on the drawings – it will be interesting for your son to flick through them later in life.

Use dolls, action figures, cuddly toys, hand puppets...

In the same way as you use a phrase to start a story and a drawing as a beginning for a picture story, you can use any toy figure, be it a doll, an action figure, a teddy bear or a car as the starting point for a story – any toy can have its own personality and adventure.

Hand puppets have always been my favourite toy to create stories with. They have an amazing ability to engage a child in their story. They are also a good way of communicating about something that your little boy might be worried about or afraid of. By making the potential issue one that the puppet has, he is much more likely to speak about it more openly than if you would ask him directly.

Toys and hand puppets can even be used to introduce a third language into your communication. If you are bilingual yourself and you know the other language your son is using (but don't normally speak it with him), then you can have one toy figure or puppet that speaks that language. This is a good way of increasing the amount of exposure to the other language if you feel it needs a boost. It will not confuse your boy, even though you speak the "wrong" language, because you are doing it on the puppet's behalf it. He will identify the toy as a speaker of the other language. It may confuse *you* to start with, but you will soon get the hang of it.

Link the activity to your child's interests

To come up with a story together or draw a picture or play with toys will work well as long your son is still interested in these activities. What to do when your creativity is called for when he is a bit older, maybe already a teenager? Trickery ("the kitten only speaks my language"), stories ("oh, come on, Mum!") or even pleading will no longer do, so you have to come up with something else to motivate him to continue using and getting better at your language. Motivation is the mother (and father for all I know) of all learning. If you can come up with ways of creating compelling enough reasons for him, you will soon be back on track again.

Creativity

Think of what your son is interested in. If he is into music or films – introduce him to movies or songs in your language. YouTube is a great place to start looking. If he is into computer games, find some in your language – he will probably not appreciate the ones you find, but show him the way to explore others.

If there is a specific hobby he likes, look for books, magazines, YouTube videos or websites on the topic. If it is sports he is interested in, find material on the type of sport he likes. Again, the internet is our best assistant in these searches.

Remember that the best way for him to learn is to use the language with another person. Reading about a topic or watching a video doesn't necessarily improve his language that effectively, but it will keep his interest going. The ideal way is to get him to engage in a conversation to make the language stick. If you find it difficult to lead these discussions yourself – maybe you don't know the topic or you are not the right discussion partner for your son – try to find someone his age who he could share his interest with. You would, however, need to find someone who is monolingual in your language; otherwise the likelihood is that they will start talking the majority language together.

If monolingual same aged youngsters are hard to find where you live, then the next time you visit your "home" country, try to find, for example, a sports club he could visit while you are there. Hopefully he could make some friends and they could keep contact via Skype, Google+ or some other way which allows them to chat to each other without your bank balance being affected too much.

7.1.3 Keep it simple

Creativity is all too often made to sound like something that you need artistic talent or great inspiration for. I don't think this is correct. Every one of us is creative in one way or another in our daily lives. You may not think you are creative – it might be called "thinking out of the box" – finding an alternative solution or coming up with a different way of doing something. The way to make the concept of creativity less daunting is to keep it simple.

You don't need expensive materials to be creative

You already have things in your home that will help you with being creative. Having an open mind is the first and probably the most important part of getting your creative juices flowing – a totally free commodity. Stories can be created out of nothing: you simply need to take the initiative and your girl's imagination will take care of the rest. If you have a phone that can do voice recording, or a laptop with a microphone, do capture the stories you create together.

Paper, pens and crayons can be found in any child's toolbox. Use magazines and newspapers to create your picture stories and storyboards. Any toy can take on a new personality and go on a new adventure, helping you to pass on your language to your little girl.

Relax, don't force it!

One thing is sure about being creative – you can't force it. You can't decide: "I will now create something interesting" – it doesn't work like that. Remember to be open-minded and let your daughter lead you, or draw on her interests. So relax, look around you: what have you got handy to help you come up with new ideas? Ask your daughter what she would like to do – what would be fun?

If you feel short of ideas, think of what has worked in the past. What did you do when you had a fun or exciting time together? When you come up with something, find a way to combine the activity with a lot of communication. You could also think of someone who you consider to be creative and good with children. What would this person do?

Keep in mind, you are not setting off to create a piece of art and you are not aiming to be the next J K Rowling. What you are doing

Creativity

is helping your girl learn your language. However, for all I know, you might end up with some terrific stories that others would like to hear as well.

Another important thing is to be flexible. Don't plan too much or have a specific goal in mind. If your story only lasts a few minutes – fine! By all means, if you are looking to introduce some specific vocabulary, do so, but don't do it at the cost of your daughter's interest in the story.

7.2 When creativity is called for

There are times in every multilingual family when the ordinary, normal routine isn't enough to keep the momentum going and you need an extra boost to reach your goal of raising your son to become bilingual.

Motivation is of utmost importance for your son to continue to use and enhance all his language skills. The tools to motivate him will naturally depend on his age and interests, and you will know best what will inspire him. I will, however, give some ideas on what you could do to encourage him.

Then there are those situations where you feel you have hit a brick wall and nothing seems to work and you are afraid all your hard work will come to nothing. This is how it can feel when your son answers you in the "wrong" language. The challenge might come in the form of a change in routines and you not having enough time to provide the necessary exposure to your language. During the teenage years, anything can suddenly change and your son might find your language boring, too difficult, old-fashioned or uninteresting. The challenges you might meet as a multilingual family will be unique to you, and you will be the expert on solving them, but I will offer some thoughts on how to tackle different situations.

To offer the motivation your son needs to want to learn your language, try to make learning fun. If you are enjoying yourself, you learn better and you want more of it. Having fun together also strengthens your relationship with your little boy. Not to mention that laughing in general is good for you: according to the proverb "a minute of laughter prolongs your life by five minutes" – that's a good investment if there ever was one.

Games are a good way of learning languages and you probably already know some of them. Coming up with your own games allows you to introduce a specific vocabulary to your playing. The games don't have to be elaborate and you can make almost anything into a playful game, including everyday tasks.

Motivation

How best to motivate your daughter to use and learn more of your language will, of course, depend on her age, interests and personality. There is no one way which would be the right one and always work for everyone. You know your daughter so you are the expert on what is the best way to engage her. The following suggestions will hopefully inspire you to come up with your own types of motivation techniques.

When your daughter is a toddler, having fun is the best motivation for her. If she learns to connect your language with fun, she will be naturally drawn to using it. This is the reason why I am not a fan of parents using a variation of the *Mixed Use* method who only revert to their native language when they have something serious to say or get upset with their children. It might be effective, in that children get a kind of respect for the language in terms of "When mum speaks her native language, you know she is really angry", but that is not the kind of association you want your daughter to have with your language. Later on in this section, you will find ideas on how to create positive connections with your language and keep it fun.

If you do need some extra motivation for your toddler, then I am not averse to using rewards (or bribes, if you prefer that term). Use whatever way you know will spur your daughter on. Maybe she likes

Creativity

charts where she can get a sticker every time she does well and something nice after a certain amount of stickers. Maybe she can have her favourite food if she manages to stick to your language all morning, or you can play her favourite game if she learns a song in your language.

As discussed in the chapters about the DOs and the DO NOTs of multilingual parenting, I don't believe that you should demand that your daughter speaks your language, instead make it so compelling for her that she wants to do it.

I do think you should be honest with your daughter, but at the same time, if a little white lie can keep you on track, I am not averse to using that method. It worked for us – remember Pricken, the Swedish-speaking kitten in chapter 3.4?

When your daughter grows up and understands reasoning a bit better, you can speak to her about the advantages of knowing your language. Apart from the obvious ones of being able to communicate with the extended family and other benefits to do with communication, thinking, career and even health (the last one probably doesn't fly with young people, but you can give it a try), knowing another language will give her more options later in life. She will have a greater choice of where she wants to study, work and live, as she won't have a language dilemma if she chooses a country where your language is spoken. You can find a list of main benefits in section 2 at the start of the book.

My younger daughter Daniela is, at the time of writing this book, studying medicine and once she has completed her studies, she has the choice of working as a doctor somewhere where English or Swedish is one of the required languages. As she is also working on improving her passive Finnish knowledge to become one of her active languages, this will add one more option for her. Her Punjabi will be a great help for her working in the UK.

Tackling challenges

Parenting always has its challenges, which differ depending on your child's age and your family's circumstances. Raising your son to become bilingual does add one more variable to the family life, and it can bring with it some surprises and situations that you need to deal with.

Despite your best efforts and a well thought-out *Family Language Plan*, you may find that at times you don't get enough one-on-one time with your son or that some other part of your plan doesn't work out the way you thought it would do. As long as you are aware of these situations, there is usually something you can do to increase the exposure.

The first resource to turn to is normally your extended family – if your parents live nearby and don't already play a big part in the *Family Language Plan*, ask them if they could spend some more time with their grandson. Maybe he could stay with them over school holidays or they could come and visit more often. What about the rest of the family – could they help with childminding combined with language exposure? Maybe you can find a family among your friends who speak the same language and you could offer to look after their child in return for them looking after your son at times? A costlier option is to look into getting an au pair to help you with both childcare and language exposure.

Another situation where your creativity might be called for is when your son goes to school and the exposure to the majority language significantly increases. He will get new friends who might only speak one language; maybe he starts a new hobby – again, in the majority language. It is important that you make sure your language doesn't get side-lined at this crucial point in your boy's life. Find ways to motivate him to keep speaking your language.

Creativity

Motivation is also badly needed if you find yourself in a situation where he decides not to speak your language anymore. This is undeniably a difficult situation for you, but don't get offended. If you handle the situation calmly and firmly, the phase will pass. To get him back on track, try to arrange some time in a monolingual environment in your language. Perhaps a trip "back home" during the school holidays?

Then there's the potential teenage rebellion time when everything is either "Boring!" or "Not interesting!" or "Only for old people!" or "Not for me!" At this stage of your son's life, your creativity can really be put to the test. To keep going, remind yourself of the reasons why you want him to become bilingual. It might not feel like it when you are in the thick of it, but he will one day thank you for being persistent and coming up with ways of motivating him to keep going.

Fun and games

Several times in this book, I have talked about the importance on having fun when passing on your language to your daughter. In a busy family with children, jobs and chores to juggle with, I know that not all days are filled with joy. Sometimes it does feel *all but* fun and you are simply looking to survive to the next day without blowing your fuses due to exhaustion. And I am asking you to make all this fun?! Well, I am, and I am trying to help you come up with ways of doing it without having to spend too much of your time or money while doing so.

There are several reasons why I am so keen on bringing in the fun factor when you are passing on your language. Learning is so much easier when you enjoy it. If you come up with a fun way of, for example, learning new words together, your daughter will want to do it again and again, increasing her vocabulary each time. She will also gain a lot of positive memories connected to your language, and a good laugh together is a great way to strengthen your relationship.

When your daughter still wants to spend as much time as possible with you, having fun together is a good way to motivate her. When she grows up, the enjoyment might come from different forms of activities – ones she can share with her friends or do on her own.

For as long as you have her undivided attention, however, make the most of the time to give her a good start in her language development. Playing games together is an activity you can both enjoy. By games, I don't mean board or other games that require you to set up all the paraphernalia, but simple activities or even simple everyday chores. I am a great believer in allowing children to take part in simple tasks as soon as they are able to. When they are small, they are so keen to help you with anything they can, and I think that is a crucial time for them to learn to participate in jobs around the home. If you don't involve them at this stage, then I am afraid you shouldn't be surprised if they don't show any interest when they are older. Sorry, this is a bit of a diversion, but I hope you can see the point I am making. Your daughter can help you empty the washing machine and you can learn names for colours, garments, parts of clothing and so on while doing it. In the garden, she can get to know the names of flowers and insects – better have a dictionary handy, as you will probably get asked about items you have no idea what they are called.

Another game you can play is "Word of the Day": decide on a word (or a group of words) that you are going to learn on a specific day and then try to use the words as often as you can. Your daughter, of course, gets a sticker or a point every time she manages to put one of the words in a phrase. "I Spy" is a great game for learning words – choose a letter for that day then point out anything that starts with that letter. When your girl is a bit older and has learnt to read, you can use sticky notes on items at home to remind her of what they are called (I know, it does get a bit messy after a while and visitors might wonder what you are up to). Make it even more fun by mixing the notes up and ask her to put them in their right places. Children love treasure trails – they do take a bit of planning and organising, but they are worth it once in a while. Hide her rewards, birthday or other presents, and then write clues on notes, one leading to another. The final one will reveal what she is looking for.

Creativity

The list of simple games you can play together to enhance your daughter's language is endless – in previous sections I have mentioned stories, role plays with toys, pictures and storyboards. Don't forget one of my favourites: hand puppets.

7.3 Finding inspiration

So you have exhausted your own creativity resources and want to do something different to motivate your son to learn your language. Maybe you are looking to make it more fun, or perhaps you have a bit of dilemma with your little prince as he only wants to speak one language, the "wrong" one, with you. Where do you go for inspiration, support and advice to come up with new ideas?

The internet is the place to start to quickly find some new ideas. There is a vast amount of information available to you in the form of websites, forums and blogs dedicated to multilingual parenting. You can find stories, music, children's programmes and educational material in several languages.

While the internet is a true treasure trove, don't forget the traditional media like books, newspapers and magazines. Depending on your TV service provider, you might find programmes in your language, and you can listen to radio stations on the TV as well. Radio stations in different languages can also be found on the internet.

Other multilingual families can be of great help. They understand your situation and might even have experienced the same challenges as you. With them you can share your experiences and ask for advice. Maybe you can also swap books, magazines and other material that will help you.

Then there is, of course, your extended family and circle of friends – ask them for their thoughts on what you need help with. They may not be experts on the issues that are on your mind, but talking about the matter might help you see other solutions or get some inspiration for your quest to raise your son to speak the family's languages.

The internet

Like with any dilemma, nowadays the internet is the place to start to quickly find some new ideas.

There are several websites dedicated to multilingual parenting and many of them have forums where you can find new ideas. Any challenge you are facing while raising your daughter to become bilingual has most likely been experienced by other parents as well. If you have a specific question that you can't find information on, why not start a thread yourself? In the **References and other Resources** section at the end of the book, you will find a list of useful sites – for an updated list of available resources, please check the website at www.multilingualparenting.com.

In addition to providing advice and shared experiences from other multilingual families, the internet is great for finding music in your language. Type in your favourite children's songs into a search engine or YouTube and soon you are likely to come across a version of the song your mother or grandmother sung to you when you were little. Listen to the music with your daughter, and even better, learn to sing it together. If she is too little to learn it, sing it as a lullaby when she goes to sleep.

There are also a lot of audio books available on the net. These are a useful supplement (not replacement) if you find that your daughter is not getting enough exposure to one of her languages. Remember that you can also make your own audio books by recording a story while you are reading it. These recordings will be a treasure not only for you and your children, but for generations to come.

Look up the web page of a broadcasting company of a country where your language is spoken. Most of them have good quality programmes

Creativity

suitable to watch together with your little girl. Again, remember that interaction is the key. The idea is to find a programme and then watch it together. I know, sometimes you will have to leave her to enjoy it on her own (all parents do), but please don't make it the only way she watches the programmes.

Material aimed at schoolchildren in the country of your language is a brilliant support for your daughter's learning – again, use the search engines to locate educational programmes, exercises and games. When your daughter is a bit older, she can use these sites to improve her reading and writing skills. However, don't leave her fully to her own devices; she will need your encouragement and help.

There are also many radio stations that you can stream over the internet. Find out when they have children's programmes and tune in to listen together. Radio is not perhaps the most interesting of the media for today's children, so you might find that you have to make it more exciting. For example, if it is a story, take on one of the characters and play it out while listening. If you don't find anything suitable to listening together to, I am sure *you* will enjoy the programmes and get inspiration from them.

I have already mentioned YouTube with regards to finding music, but it is so much more than that. You can search for anything on it – use your language to search for a specific topic. You can get ideas for all kinds of activities: why not look up how to build a hut or a rocket (the cardboard box variety), how to cook a delicious dessert or how to grow vegetables? Choose something your daughter is already interested in and you will be on to a winner.

Books and other media

The internet has taken over many of the roles that traditional media used to have. Entertainment, education, news, recipes, manuals - you name it, the internet is now the place to go for any type of information. Young people apparently rather look on the internet for how to iron a shirt instead of asking their parents or grandparents. Sad in a way, but that's the way it goes.

This doesn't mean that you should disregard the traditional media when you are bringing up your son to speak your language. Books are very important in the language learning process. Introduce your boy to books at an early age. Ideally make them part of your daily routine. Read to him from the day he's born (if you are the mother, then please rest and ask the father to do the reading that day!).

Reading will become connected with special moments in his life, something he will look forward to. He will also learn to appreciate books, something which will be beneficial to him throughout his life and especially when he goes to school. If he gets used to the world of books, he will always have something to do – no panic if the internet is down, the computer is broken or he is stuck somewhere without any other distractions. A good book can keep him occupied for hours. Reading is a great way to enhance your vocabulary and learn about new things, both for children and adults. By the way, did I mention that I like books?

Books can be expensive if you buy them all, so borrow from friends and family. If you have a public library nearby, visit it to see what they have. If they don't have books in your language, ask if they can order some for you. Make it a habit to take your son with you on the library visits – libraries are no longer the quiet places they once used to be, so children are welcome. Many of them also organise activities around books such as reading hours and author visits.

Magazines and newspapers are cheaper than books to buy, though a subscription would set you back a lot more. They can, however, be used for other activities once you have read them – create storyboards with them or use the pictures to illustrate your own stories. If that sounds like a little bit too much to do, then get magazines you like yourself and read them for your own enjoyment. Your son might get interested in them too (this depends, of course, on what kind of magazines you like). If he is a little baby, read out loud to him – small babies don't mind what you read to them, they love hearing your voice and learn the language at the same time.

Television is not so much appreciated among parenting experts, but you can still find good programmes out there. If you are the minority language parent, it might be a bit more difficult depending on where in the world you live, but on some satellite TV channels you can get programmes in a variety of languages. Also check the radio stations that might be available. The best way to find some suitable programmes is to plan ahead and check what is available, then organise the time when you can watch or listen together with your son. Again, if that sounds like too much hassle, check for podcasts in your language, or possible TV catch-up websites.

Other multilingual families

No one will understand your dilemmas and challenges better than other parents in families with more than one language. Though their language combinations might not be the same as yours, the principles are still the same and usually the problems are as well. Don't be afraid to ask for advice from other families if you feel stuck; they will be happy to share their experiences – wouldn't you be, if you knew you could help someone in a similar situation? Don't forget to check the forums at www.multilingualparenting.com.

You can go online to seek advice in many forums, but if you can arrange to meet a similar family face-to-face, all the better. Getting to know other families that raise their children to speak their family's languages gives you an invaluable support group that you can turn to when you are in need of some encouragement. Speak with parents who have been successful at passing on their languages to their children. Ask them what they think was the crucial factor to their success. Also speak to parents in families where the children didn't learn the family's languages – what did they do differently?

If you can, arrange to meet up with more than one multilingual family at the same time – you could then not only share experiences, tips and tricks, but also arrange swaps: books, magazines, DVDs and so on.

Another idea is to arrange play dates for your children, or agree to look after each other's children in turn – giving you some spare time as well. For a play date, it is beneficial if you can arrange it with a child who *only* speaks your family's minority language – it is a great incentive for your daughter to use her language.

If there are many families with the same minority language, then a playgroup would be a great idea. This would, of course, need some more organising, but perhaps there is a parent that would be happy to start a group and others could either pay towards the costs or help along.

Extended family and friends

If you are grappling with something and have run out of ideas, who do you turn to? I don't know about you, but for me it is my friends and the extended family.

They might not be able to give you advice with something specific on how to raise your son to become bilingual, but discussing the matter with someone else usually clarifies your own mind and you may then come up with a solution yourself.

For ideas on activities you can do with your son, your parents and grandparents can speak about what they did as children. Older relatives are usually very pleased if someone comes and asks them about their childhood and stories from their lives – remember to have your recorder handy.

If you are noticing that your son is not getting as much exposure to your language as he should to ensure he becomes an active speaker of your language, again, ask your family or friends that speak the

Creativity

language. They might be able to help or know someone that could spend some time with your son on a regular basis. The more speakers of your language your son comes in contact with, the better. No two persons speak alike – their vocabulary is not the same and their accent may slightly differ. Communicating with different people is good for your son's understanding of the language, making him used to hearing things said in ways not identical to your own.

You can also ask your relatives and friends in your home country to send you materials that will help your son with his language learning – ask for magazines, old schoolbooks, films or music, for example.

What next?

Being a parent is not easy at the best of times and you will frequently have challenges thrown in your way. When this happens, it is important to stay resourceful and not to give up. Use your creativity to come up with ways to motivate and make learning your language fun for your daughter. Whenever you feel stuck or are looking for ideas, reread this section – hopefully it will spur you on.

So far we have come across five of the seven Cs that you need to be able to sail through on your multilingual family journey: **Communication**, **Confidence**, **Commitment**, **Consistency** and **Creativity**. In the next section, I will tackle the fascinating topic of **Culture** and why it is so important that you cherish your culture, wherever you come from.

8 Culture

Why have I included a section on culture in a book about bringing up your child to speak more than one language? To me, language and culture always go together; one comes with the other and it is difficult to have one without the other. I like the following definition of the word 'culture':

> *"Culture is the characteristics of a particular group of people,*
> *defined by everything from language, religion,*
> *cuisine, social habits, music and arts."*
> (Kim Ann Zimmermann, LiveScience)

Language is mentioned first in the list of culture components, and rightly so, as culture is to a high degree conveyed through language in some form. Visual arts, dance, food and instrumental music (among others) are also important parts of our culture, but language is the main way we learn about it. Note that being a fluent bilingual does not automatically mean that you are also bicultural – you may know the language and something about its traditions and history, but still not feel part of the culture.

It is important to be familiar with your own cultural background to fully know who you are. To understand your culture and to take part in its traditions, you need to know the language it is conveyed in. Translations of books, poems or jokes are never the same as the original. They are mostly of a good quality and certainly interesting reading, but they will always be an interpretation by the person who translated them.

As a parent, it is vital that you are a good role model to your son. For him to be interested in your culture and background, you need to show that you are proud of it. Being proud of your culture not only gives you confidence but also gains the respect of your son. Remember that it is not only a language you are passing on to the

Culture

*"Culture is the widening of the mind
and of the spirit."*

- Jawaharlal Nehru

next generation but also the culture and a positive attitude to it. Your family stories and traditions will live on through your children and grandchildren.

8.1 Language and culture go hand in hand

Language and culture are so intertwined that you can't really have one without the other. When you are passing on your language to your daughter, you are not only teaching her to speak your language, but you are also opening the doors to your cultural background for her. Of course, she could learn about the culture even if she didn't speak the language, but it wouldn't be the same.

If you live far away from your home country, and might not even have extended family around you, it can at first feel difficult to know how you will manage to pass on your cultural heritage, but today's abundance of media makes it possible in different ways.

When Minna and Daniela were small and we were still living in Finland, it wasn't easy to find material for them in Punjabi (this was well before YouTube and downloadable films). There weren't even many other families where Punjabi was spoken. So I remember how happy I was to get hold of a video of a Punjabi-speaking comedian, Mehar Mittal. This video became one of the girls' favourite programmes alongside the lovely Moomin episodes which were either in Swedish or Finnish.

Literature, music, films, theatre, TV

By consciously including films, music and literature into the upbringing of your son, you give him a sound understanding of your culture. I have mentioned the importance of books before and I shall not miss the chance to reiterate how beneficial reading is to learning languages. Start with reading fairy tales and other children's books to him, as well as rhymes and poems. Help him to start reading himself.

153

Continue to comics and magazines and then to go on to novels. If you haven't been much of a reader yourself, you might even discover a whole new thrilling world through books yourself.

Sing lullabies to him when he's a baby and sing together when he starts speaking. If he is interested in some particular piece of music, find the lyrics and learn them together.

Children love theatre, so if you get the chance to go and watch a child-friendly play, don't miss the chance. This might not be easy if you are no longer living in the country of your language, but do go and see any visiting companies or small local productions.

I've touched on films earlier and with so many films in different languages available online, it has become much easier to find them. When your son has learnt to read, look for films that have subtitles in your language. Some TV service providers also offer subtitles in different languages for any programme, so look out for those as well.

Bilingual doesn't automatically mean bicultural

There is a distinction to be made between being bilingual and being bicultural. Speaking more than one language or dialect makes you bilingual, but to be bicultural you need to have a deeper understanding and a sense of belonging to the culture of the people speaking the language. If you learn a new language as an adult, you do become bilingual, but unless you spend a lot of time in the cultural surroundings of a language, it is unlikely you become bicultural.

It will take quite a lot of effort and time to adopt another culture when you are an adult. Children, however, will pick this up as they go along, as long as they are exposed to the cultural influences. You do want your daughter to feel at home in your culture, so this is why you should involve her in it.

8.2 Knowing your culture helps you understand your identity

When you grow up in the place where your culture is the dominant one, you don't pay much attention to the fact that you are growing up as a member of the culture – it is just what happens. But if you or your family have moved to a different area, it becomes more prevalent. Food, traditions and customs gain a more important role in your life. You also have to put in a bit more effort to keep these aspects of your life alive.

In my opinion, when you move to another country (or different cultural surroundings), you should make an effort to integrate in the new culture. You can, however, do this without losing your own cultural identity. The culture of your family will always be with you in one way or another and it is important for your understanding of your own identity. When you are teaching your son your language and introducing him to the culture, you are giving him a good foundation in life.

Culture

One of the main reasons for us moving from Finland to England was to give Minna and Daniela the chance to learn to know their father's culture better. Of course, the best place to soak in the culture would have been Punjab, but that was not a viable option for us. England has a large Punjabi community and there was much more on offer for our daughters to connect with the culture. They both attended Punjabi classes and learnt to master reading as well. Our move did mean that I had to leave my home country, but rather that than them having to "find their roots" later in life.

Sometime when you use the word "culture", people think about highbrow, expensive art or exclusive music performances, but they are just a small part of our culture. Others associate culture with "old fashioned" stuff, which is equally incorrect. Our history and traditions are, of course, an important part of our culture, but so is everything that is happening today – modern trends, new types of food, clothing, TV programmes and so on.

So when you are including as much of this as possible in your son's upbringing, you support his self-image in that he knows his background and understands the bigger picture of where he comes from.

8.3 Be proud of your culture

To successfully pass on any values, attitudes, habits, traditions or even a language, as a parent you have to believe in them and be proud of them yourself. If you don't appreciate what you are trying to pass on to your daughter, the success rate will decrease. If you are trying to nurture certain values in your daughter, then you have to live according to them yourself. "Don't do as I do, do as I say," doesn't work in the long run. Therefore, it is important that you show your pride in your own culture. If you ignore or belittle its value, so will she.

With pride, I don't mean a we-are-better-than-everybody else attitude, but a confident joy in your own culture. Independent of where you come from, or even if you have had to leave your home country against your will, there is always something genuine and original to be proud of in your culture. By showing your pride in it, you are being a positive role model to your daughter, so that she can be confident in her own identity. When I say "showing your pride", I mean exactly that. Words are not enough – you have to behave accordingly.

If you feel uncomfortable of the thought of being proud of your background and heritage, then I would suggest you think about why it is so. Are you harbouring some negative beliefs about the value of your own culture, and if yes, what are they based on? We all have things in our cultural history that we might not be that proud of, but this shouldn't stop you from finding the aspects of your culture that you do want to cherish and pass on to your daughter.

When you share your cultural background with your daughter and teach her to be proud of it, it will give her confidence in life. Confidence is particularly important when growing up, especially if you are a bit different from others – which many children from multilingual families are. Maybe not always in how they look, but at least in what languages they know. Also when you are positively confident about yourself and your identity, you will gain others' respect.

Language is the key to getting to know a culture, so that alone would be a good enough reason to make sure your little girl grows up to speak your language.

8.4 Pass on your cultural heritage

If you were not convinced of the importance of your cultural heritage for your son before, I hope I have managed to persuade you. How to pass on your culture without making it seem boring, old-fashioned, tedious, whatever-he-doesn't-like to your son?

Culture

When he's small, he will go along with you – if you are enthusiastic, so will he be. Engage him in traditions, music and films when he is small, and it will most likely keep him interested when he gets into his teenage years. If you notice that he is not too keen on something, discuss it with him. Explain the custom, why you are doing something in a specific way on a certain day or with certain people – you will probably learn something along the way as well.

Family stories are a great and entertaining way of giving your son an insight into your family culture. Record them and, if you have the time, write them down to make a family history book. Your older relatives will have so many interesting tales to give you and your son a vivid picture of how life was in the past.

However, as I have mentioned before, culture is not only about history, old traditions and past works of art. Culture is as much about what is happening today, all the modern trends in your culture's environment. When you try to keep on top of that, your cultural education quest stays fresh and interesting – automatically more appealing, especially to teenagers.

Showing pride in your culture is vital, but do keep it real. Though you highly appreciate your culture, don't idealise it to your son. I know this is something that expats sometimes fall foul of – remembering only the good things about your old country and omitting all the not so good aspects. You don't want your son to have a negative experience when he visits your country, so be realistic about things that might not be ideal.

The absolute best way to pass on your culture along with the language is if you can regularly arrange visits to your home country. I know this might not always be financially viable, but give it your best shot. If you don't have the chance to travel that often, then you could consider letting your son travel with other families when he is a bit older. If possible, arrange for him to take part in some activities he is already interested in during his visit. Spending time with other children of the same age will considerably improve his language skills and his cultural understanding.

What more?

Language and culture go hand in hand. By passing on your language to your daughter, you are automatically also sharing your culture with her. If you want her to not only become bilingual, but also bicultural – feeling at ease and at home in any of the family's cultures – then make your culture part of the process.

We are nearing the destination port of our multilingual parenting journey. Six of the seven Cs have been successfully conquered: *Communication*, *Confidence*, *Commitment*, *Consistency*, *Creativity* and *Culture* – what is there left to do? Prepare to *Celebrate* your and your children's efforts to pass on the family languages to the next generation.

Culture

"The more you praise and celebrate your life, the more there is in life to celebrate."

- Oprah Winfrey

9 Celebration

Every achievement deserves a celebration. Learning another language is certainly a good reason for a pat on the back. There are many things in our lives that we take for granted, speaking more than one language being one of them, and I think it is high time to celebrate the fact that we can communicate across cultural and geographical borders.

The everyday way to celebrate your family's and children's language skills is to never miss a chance to give positive feedback. When your son shows progress in his learning, make sure to praise him and show how happy you are about it. Also give him visible signs of your appreciation (stickers on a chart, a 'well done' badge...), as a reminder for the whole family of how well you are doing.

Keeping a *Language Success Diary* is a great way of celebrating all tiny steps on the way to becoming a bilingual for your son. Writing down the new words and phrases he learns as well as saving audio and video clips of his progress will create an excellent source of inspiration for you when you feel it is not going so well. It will also spur him and following generations on to keep up the multilingual tradition in the family.

It wouldn't be a celebration without a party, would it? Make it an annual celebration of the family's languages and cultures and invite others to share the event with you. Choose a day in the year that fits your family – maybe combine it with a national holiday in your country or some milestone you have reached as a family. If you have moved as a family, it could be the day you first arrived in the new country. There is, of course, a natural choice for another yearly celebration, which is the 21st of February, which is the International Mother Language Day, as recognised by the United Nations.

Celebration

9.1 Positive feedback and motivation

When it comes to celebration, start with the small easy things you can do every day and make them a habit. Celebration doesn't have to be something big – simply saying "well done!" to acknowledge a new word or phrase or correctly formed sentence will give your daughter a warm feeling inside. Quite often we think that someone has done something commendable, but we fail to say it out loud. Giving positive feedback on the progress that you notice in your daughter's language skills will motivate her to learn more.

Remember to always phrase your feedback in a positive way. This may sound like an obvious statement, but it is easy to get it wrong. Let's say, for example, that your daughter has been using your language less and you want to commend her on using it in a certain situation. Don't say: "Great that you didn't say that in the wrong language!" but instead pick up the fact that she did speak your language: "Wonderful that you knew how to say that!" Positive feedback should always point towards the goal, not mention past mistakes.

Motivation is vitally important for any learning process, and it can come in many different forms. I firmly believe in positive motivation, whatever the age of a child. Negative consequences or threats will never achieve a positive learning experience and rarely result in a balanced, lasting skill. I know there are differing opinions among parenting experts on this – some say we spoil our children if we praise them too much. As long as you praise for a genuine reason, I can't see the harm in doing so. I do, however, know how demoralising it can be *not* to be recognised for something you have achieved.

A 'well done' chart is an excellent way of celebrating your daughter's progress when she's small. Use the chart frequently and generously, adding stars, points or smiley faces for new words and phrases. When her skills progress, reward her for using her languages more and in different situations. If she has been using a language mainly at home, recognise her efforts when she speaks the language outside her familiar environment. Give her positive feedback on anything that you feel is moving her towards the goal of becoming an active bilingual.

In addition to the chart, create a set of certificates and prizes that she can have after a certain amount of achievements. Arrange a bigger celebration when she reaches certain milestones in her language development – maybe a visit "back home" could be part of your celebrations?

The way you give feedback should, of course, be age-appropriate. You will know best what works for your daughter when she grows older and a sticker chart is no longer interesting or words of encouragement are not enough. Draw on her interests when you want to celebrate her language successes – arrange a trip to your home country for her and let her decide what she wants to do. Maybe she would like to visit a different part of the country or join in some activities that she is interested in. Accept that she might want to do these things on her own – an important part of growing up and becoming the confident bilingual you want her to be.

9.2 Keep a Language Success Diary

When children grow up, they learn things amazingly quickly, and if you don't write it down as and when it happens, it will soon be forgotten. Therefore I suggest that you keep a diary for your son's language progress – I call this a *Language Success Diary*. By naming the diary a 'success', it also becomes a bit of a self-fulfilling prophecy: your family's language journey will be a success.

The *Language Success Diary* can be in written form of a traditional diary, or in digital form to be kept as a file on the computer. The advantage of making it digital is that you can add video and audio clips to it to make it even more comprehensive. I know this sounds a bit like hard work and much to do for your already busy schedule, but it will be worth every minute you spend on it when you revisit it

Celebration

afterwards. Not to mention how grateful your son will be when he grows up – believe me, there will come a time when he will want to see how he developed when he was small.

So what should you record in a *Language Success Diary*? The first words in each language, followed by phrases and full sentences in each language are, of course, the obvious ones. However, don't stop at the first few utterances – keep recording new words as and when he uses them. You will find it interesting to see which words he learns in each language. Also note any of his own words that he makes up for things he doesn't yet know the new name for.

Alongside the specific words and phrases, also keep a diary of how he develops as a bilingual. Record when you first notice that he seems to be aware that he is using two languages and when he first translates a word for someone (this will happen sooner than you think).

> *I remember writing about the first time Minna took on the task of being a translator. She was a year and a few months old when we were on a ferry on our way to visit friends and family in Sweden. She was in her dad's arms and we all stood looking out across the open sea, watching seabirds trying to catch some fish. Her dad pointed out the water and the birds and said the Punjabi words 'pani' and 'panchi'. Minna then turned to me and said the words in Finnish: 'vesi' and 'lintu'. For me, this was a remarkable moment not only in that she could translate, but that she was already aware of the intricacies of language use and knew that she and her dad were using a language I didn't understand. To include me in the conversation, she explained the discussion in the language she spoke with me.*

Also record how much your son is using of each language. In this way, the *Language Success Diary* will also help you to keep track of his progress as a whole in each language, and it will give you an idea of how much he is learning. If it is less than you would have expected, then revisit the *Family Language Plan* and check that he is still getting enough exposure for each of his languages.

Don't forget to document the way he learns to write as well – his first stories in his own handwriting will be a great treasure in years to come. By saving some of his written texts every month or so, you will get a nice overview of how his writing progresses.

Fill the diary with any observations you make about his language development. Also record anything that you do together to support his language development. Which games does he enjoy? What are his favourite stories? Which books do you read to him over and over again? Which songs do you like singing together? Which children's rhymes have you been reciting together?

Reading through your son's *Language Success Diary* will give you inspiration to continue when you are going through a difficult patch and you feel that one of his languages is taking backstage and not progressing in the way you would like to. This could be, for example, after he starts school and uses the majority language a lot more and maybe seems not that keen on speaking your family's minority language. Open the diary and read through the notes that you have made until then – remember the successes you have had and everything that you have done to ensure he becomes an active bilingual. This, I am sure, will give you the encouragement you need to keep on going and finding ways around any obstacles you may meet.

9.3 Arrange a party!

If you are a bilingual like me, I think you can agree with me that we take our language skills for granted all too often. Languages become such an integral part of our lives that we don't think of them as anything special. Knowing more than one language is, however, something that we should show more appreciation for – by doing so, we are also contributing to raising the value of language skills. Monolinguals won't do it for us, will they?

Celebration

Celebrate the fact that you are a multilingual family and that your children will grow up to increase the understanding between societies and cultures! Conflicts often arise due to not enough or inadequate communication and I do believe that if more people knew more languages, there would be less misunderstanding in the world. As multilingual and multicultural families, we should show our pride in our language skills in any way we can. This way, we will also be good role models for generations to come.

A proper celebration calls for a party, doesn't it? I think that all multilingual families should celebrate their languages and cultures at least twice a year. Why twice, you may ask. Well there is a good reason for that. I think every family should choose one day that is significant to them and their languages. It could be a national holiday in your country or some other day that is befitting.

The second party for the year could be a common one for all multilingual families in the world and the natural choice of day is the 21st of February, which the United Nations General Assembly has chosen as the International Mother Language Day. "Languages are the most powerful instruments of preserving and developing our tangible and intangible heritage," is a quote from the International Mother Language Day website and I couldn't agree more.

So what should you do for your party? Do whatever makes you feel happy: invite all the family and friends. Maybe you can have a joint party with other multilingual families. Food would, of course, play a vital role in the celebration – what a fantastic chance to serve your favourite dishes to each other, especially if there are families from many different cultures involved.

Since there are several families coming together, use the opportunity to swap books, DVDs, magazines, toys and, of course, experiences. Share with other multilingual parents what has gone well but also where you have had challenges and how you overcame them. Maybe you can have a "storytelling corner" where older relatives can speak about what they did as children. For the teenagers, you might want to arrange something more in line with their interests – maybe a room where they can watch films? Even better, ask them to come up with ideas for the party and then engage them to plan and take part in the activities.

Play traditional games from your culture, both to have fun and to pass them on to the next generation. Arrange lots of entertainment for the children, as you wish for them to be enjoying themselves and to want to take part in years to come.

Music, dancing and singing belong to a good party. Make printouts for songs so everyone can take part in the singing. Before the party, ask around among your guests; there will be people who would like to perform something, be it a piece of music or a dance or something else. Maybe you can find some local talents that will come and perform especially for you – there are always fledgling artists who would love to be asked to be part of the celebrations. A good way to end a party is, of course, with everybody dancing together!

I am sure you will come up with many more ideas on how to celebrate your multilingual family and I would love to hear about them, so please get in touch via the website at www.multilingualparenting.com.

10 Summary

Together, we have sailed across the seven Cs of multilingual parenting. We have successfully **Communicated** and agreed the goals in the *Family Language Plan*. We have gathered the information we need to gain the **Confidence** in our ability to succeed in the quest to bring up bilingual children. This has allowed us to **Commit** to our common goal and ignore any doubters. We have the tools to tackle any challenges that we may encounter, and we have learnt to stay **Consistent** in our language use with our children. Our innate **Creativity** has helped us to come up with innovative ways to support and motivate our budding bilinguals. When we have wavered, we have asked for help and advice from others who have done it before. With the knowledge that language and **Culture** go hand in hand, we have also taught our children about the traditions related to the languages they know. Last but not least, we have stayed positive throughout; never losing sight of the many advantages bilingualism will bring our children. We have recorded the successes and **Celebrated** our multilingual family with relatives and friends.

We have made it to the destination port, but this is still only the start of a life-long bilingual journey for your children, and hopefully also for future generations. Good luck!

Welcome to www.multilingualparenting.com to connect and share your experiences with other multilingual families. See you there!

List of questions and where to find the answer in the book

Can I do it?

- What if I don't know my language well enough to teach it to my child? 54 62 72
- What if I teach my child something that is wrong? 63
- What if I don't know a word that my child asks me about? 114
- I am now so used to speaking the majority language that it will be difficult to use my language with my child. Should I give up? 72
- What if I can't go through with it, if I find it too hard? 73
- I am a single parent – can I raise my child to be bilingual? 41
- I am afraid of us being different as a family if we speak other languages. What to do? 93

Can my child do it?

- Will my child's language development be delayed if she/he speaks more than one language? 60
- Won't it be confusing for a child to learn two languages at once? 66
- What if my child is not linguistically talented enough to speak more than one language? 64
- My language is so difficult – will my child learn it? 68 58
- Will bilingualism cause my child to grow up being unclear about his/her identity? 155
- My child has been diagnosed as ASD – is bilingualism still an option? 77
- My child has been diagnosed with dyslexia/stutters/has a speech impediment – should we drop the other language? 79
- My second child is not learning the languages as quickly as the first one. What to do? 68 100

Child mixes languages

Child refuses to speak a language

Strategies and recommendations

Minority language

- How to motivate my child to use the minority language? 116 139 162
- Where to find resources to support the minority language? 144 185
- Will learning my language impede the learning of the majority language? 43 77 103
- What if my children decide not to talk the minority language together? 101 112
- Is watching TV programmes in the minority language helpful? 153 67
- I am the only person speaking the minority language to my child, can it still be done? 76
- I am the minority language parent - will I have to spend a lot of time supporting the language development of my child? 92
- When should we introduce the second language? 44 65

School

- My child is not a high-achiever at school – will learning two languages disadvantage her progress at school? 65
- What if my child will be bullied because of her language? 81
- Won't learning two languages detract from the ability to learn other topics at school? 63
- My child's teacher advises us to stop speaking the minority language – what should we do? 81

We can't agree on whether to raise bilingual children or not

- We are not sure whether to raise our children to be bilingual. How do we decide? 23 72 77
- My child's father/mother thinks he/she will feel left out – how to handle this? 78
- The child's father's/mother's side of the family don't accept that we raise our children to become bilingual, what to do? 79

- What if the other parent does not want our child to learn another language? 78
- My language has a low status in society – will it not be of disadvantage to my child? 76

Other concerns

- We are moving abroad – how can we retain our languages? 101
- We have just moved to a new country – should I speak the country's language with our children to help them learn it quicker? 43 77 103
- We are getting divorced – what will happen to the child's language development? 104

Family Language Plan

PART 1: Reasons

Reasons why I/we want _____ (child's name)
to become bilingual:

1 ....
....

2 ....
....

3 ....
....

4 ....
....

5 ....
....

6 ....
....

7 ....
....

8 ....
....

9 ....
....

10 ....
....

(if you have more reasons, use extra paper to complete the list)

PART 2: Fluency

Desired level of fluency and literacy.

Table A	Fluency	Reading	Writing
Language 1		Yes / No	Yes / No
Language 2		Yes / No	Yes / No
Language 3		Yes / No	Yes / No
Language 4		Yes / No	Yes / No

PART 3: Strategy and exposure

Family language strategy:..

Table B1: Exposure Language 1	Mon hours per day	Tues hours per day	Wed hours per day	Thu hours per day	Fri hours per day	Sat hours per day	Sun hours per day	TOTAL hours per week
Person Time / Place								
Person Time / Place								
Person Time / Place								
Person Time / Place								
Person Time / Place								
Total exposure for _____								

Table B2: Exposure Language 2	Mon hours per day	Tues hours per day	Wed hours per day	Thu hours per day	Fri hours per day	Sat hours per day	Sun hours per day	TOTAL hours per week
Person Time / Place								
Person Time / Place								
Person Time / Place								
Person Time / Place								
Person Time / Place								
Total exposure for _____								

Table B3: Exposure Language 3	Mon hours per day	Tues hours per day	Wed hours per day	Thu hours per day	Fri hours per day	Sat hours per day	Sun hours per day	TOTAL hours per week
Person _____ Time / Place								
Person _____ Time / Place								
Person _____ Time / Place								
Person _____ Time / Place								
Person _____ Time / Place								
Total exposure for _____								

Table B4: Exposure Language 4	Mon hours per day	Tues hours per day	Wed hours per day	Thu hours per day	Fri hours per day	Sat hours per day	Sun hours per day	TOTAL hours per week
Person _____ Time / Place								
Person Time / Place								
Person Time / Place								
Person Time / Place								
Person Time / Place								
Total exposure for _____								

Table C
Weekly exposure per language

Weekly exposure per language	(A) Total hours per week (from B1 - B4)	DIVIDED BY	(B) Waking time per week	EQUALS	(C) (A)/(B)	X 100	(D) % of exposure to language during waking time
B1 Language 1 ___							%
B2 Language 2 ___							%
B3 Language 3 ___							%
B4 Language 4 ___							%

PART 4: Support

How can the exposure time be increased? List people and activities:

Language 1. ....
....
Language 2. ....
....
Language 3. ....
....
Language 4. ....
....
Task: ....
....

PART 5: Materials

What language materials do we have available? List books, magazines, games, cartoons, movies etc.

Language 1. ....
....
Language 2. ....
....
Language 3. ....
....
Language 4. ....
....
Task: ....
....

Family Language Plan for ....
Last updated: ....

Glossary

active language skill – a language which is both understood and used

bicultural – belonging to two different cultures

bilingual – relating to more than two languages or dialects, a bilingual person is someone who uses two or more languages or dialects in their everyday lives

biliterate – a bilingual who can also read and write in more than one language

code-switching – using more than one language while talking to another bilingual

community language – the language spoken in the area you live

dominant language – the language you feel more confident in

family language – the language which is spoken in the extended family

Family Language Plan – a plan to help you stay on track while bringing up a bilingual child

family language strategy – the approach a family chooses for raising bilingual children

heritage language – the language of your family or ancestors

immersion class – class where the teaching happens in a second language

Language Success Diary – a diary of your child's language progress

majority language – the language which is spoken by the majority of the population in a community meta-linguistic awareness – understanding of the concept of a language and of its form and structures

minority language – the language which is spoken by the minority of the population in a community

Minority language at home (mL@H) – family language strategy where the family only speaks the minority language at home, and the child learns the majority language from friends, at nursery or school

Mixed use – family language strategy where the parents alternate between languages, but without a specific structure

monolingual – relating to one language, someone who only speaks one language

multilingual – relating to more than one language, often used instead of 'bilingual' when referring to ideas and concepts

One parent, one language (OPOL) – family language strategy where the parents consistently speak two different languages to the children, one of the languages may or may not be the community language

passive language skill – see 'receptive bilingualism'

receptive bilingualism – ability to understand (and maybe read) a language, but unable or unwilling to speak (or write) it

Time and place – family language strategy where children are exposed to different languages depending on time or location.

References and other Resources

Practical guides for parents

Baker, Colin. *A Parents' and Teachers' Guide to Bilingualism.* 3rd ed. Clevedon, UK: Multilingual Matters, 2007.

Barron-Hauwaert, Susan. *Bilingual Siblings.* Clevedon, UK: Multilingual Matters, 2011.

Barron-Hauwaert, Susan. *Language Strategies for Bilingual Families.* Clevedon, UK: Multilingual Matters, 2004.

Bourgogne, Annika. *Be Bilingual – Practical Ideas for Multilingual Families.* Self-published, 2013.

Cunningham, Una. *Growing up with Two Languages.* 3rd ed. London: Routledge, 2011.

Kendall, King and Mackey, Alison. *The Bilingual Edge.* New York: Harper, 2007.

Pearson, Barbara Zurer. *Raising a Bilingual Child.* New York: Living Language, 2008.

Raguenaud, Virginie. *Bilingual by Choice.* Boston: Nicholas Brealey Publishing, 2009.

Steiner, Naomi. *7 Steps to Raising a Bilingual Child.* New York: American Management Association, 2009.

Wang, Xiao-lei. *Learning to Read and Write in the Multilingual Family.* Clevedon, UK: Multilingual Matters, 2011.

General books on bilingualism

The Bilingualism Reader. Wei, Li (ed.) 2nd ed. Abingdon: Routledge, 2007.

Blackledge, Adrian and Creese, Angela. *Multilingualism.* London: Continuum, 2010.

Gardner-Chloros. *Code-switching.* Cambridge: Cambridge University Press, 2009.

Grosjean, François. *Bilingual. Life and Reality.* Cambridge: Harvard University Press, 2010.

Grosjean, François and Li, Ping. *The Psycholinguistics of Bilingualism.* Oxford: Wiley-Blackwell, 2013.

Hernandez, Arturo E. *The Bilingual Brain.* New York: Oxford University Press, 2013.

Weber, Jean-Jacques and Horner, Kristine. *Introducing Multilingualism.* Abingdon: Routledge, 2012.

Bilingual parenting websites

There are many blogs for parents of bilingual chidren. I have included the ones I read and which are regularly updated. For an up-to-date list, visit www.multilingualparenting.com

www.beingmultilingual.blogspot.co.uk
www.bilingualkidsrock.com
www.bilingualmonkeys.com
www.expatsincebirth.com
www.incultureparent.com
www.multiculturalkidblogs.com

www.multilingualliving.com
www.onraisingbilingualchildren.com
www.trilingualmama.com

General websites on language and bilingualism

For an up-to-date list, visit www.multilingualparenting.com

www.bilingualism-matters.org.uk
www.cal.org
www.languagemagazine.com
www.linguistlist.org
www.multilingualchildren.org
www.multilingual-families.eu
www.multilingual-matters.com (books)
www.psychologytoday.com/blog/life-bilingual

CPSIA information can be obtained at www.ICGtesting.com
Printed in the USA
LVOW09s2140110215

426712LV00010B/209/P